To
My Parents,
and My Brother

ACKNOWLEDGMENTS

I am deeply grateful to my advisor Dr. Baba C. Vemuri, whose guidance, encouragement and support made the completion of this work possible. I thank him for his academic as well as non-academic advice and assistance during my study at the University of Florida, and for his impressive example of integrity and academic responsibility. I wish to express sincere appreciation to my co-advisor, Dr. Hong Qin, for introducing me to the wonders of computer graphics, for patiently guiding me all the way till the end, and for assisting me in various ways. I would also like to thank Dr. Sartaj Sahni, Dr. Paul A. Fishwick and Dr. Douglas A. Cenzer for serving in my supervisory committee and advising me on various aspects of this dissertation.

My dissertation research was supported in part by the NSF grant ECS-9210648 and the NIH grant RO1-LM05944 of Dr. Vemuri, and by the NSF CAREER award CCR-9702103 and DMI-9700129 of Dr. Qin. I wish to acknowledge Dr. Tim McInerney, Dr. Gregoire Malandain, Dr. Hughes Hoppe, Dr. Kari Pulli, Dr. Dimitry Goldgof, Dr. Christina Leonard and Dr. Shang-Hong Lai for helping me at various stages of the work by providing various data sets, software and figures.

I would like to thank the faculty, staff and students of the computer and information science and engineering department, who were always there to help me.

iv

In my years with the computational vision, graphics and medical imaging group, I have enjoyed working with a set of bright students, including Yanlin Guo, Yi Cao, Li Chen, Li Wang, Shuangying Huang, Chinar Kapoor, Fengting Chen, Arun Srinivasan, Jundong Liu and Jun Ye. Special thanks goes to my long time roommates, Raja Chatterjee and Kingshuk Majumdar, for helping me in various ways during my stay at Gainesville.

Finally, I would like to thank my parents and my brother for their constant encouragement and support, for cheering me up during the hard days and for providing an ever increasing incentive to finish my graduate study. I would have been nowhere near my goals without them.

TABLE OF CONTENTS

LIST OF FIGURES

Abstract of Dissertation
Presented to the Graduate School of the University of Florida
in Partial Fulfillment of the Requirements for the
Degree of Doctor of Philosophy

A DYNAMIC FRAMEWORK FOR SUBDIVISION SURFACES

By

Chhandomay Mandal

December 1998

Chairman: Dr. Baba C. Vemuri
Cochairman : Dr. Hong Qin
Major Department: Computer and Information Science and Engineering

Subdivision surfaces are extensively used to model smooth shapes of arbitrary topology. Recursive subdivision on a user-defined initial control mesh generates a visually pleasing smooth surface in the limit. However, users have to carefully select the initial mesh and/or manipulate the control vertex positions at different levels of subdivision hierarchy to satisfy the functional and aesthetic requirements in the smooth limit surface. This modeling drawback results from the lack of direct manipulation tools for the limit surface. In this dissertation, techniques from physics-based modeling are integrated with geometric subdivision methodology, and a dynamic framework is presented for direct manipulation of the smooth limit surface generated by the subdivision schemes using physics-based "force" tools.

In a typical subdivision scheme, the user starts with an initial control mesh which is refined recursively using a fixed set of subdivision rules, and a smooth surface is produced in the limit. Most often this limit surface does not have an analytic expression, and hence poses challenging problems in incorporating mass and damping distribution functions, internal deformation energy, forces, and other physical quantities required to develop a physics-based subdivision surface model. In this dissertation, local parameterization techniques suitable for embedding the geometric subdivision surface model in a physics-based modeling framework have been developed. Specific local parameterization techniques have been fully developed for the Catmull-Clark, modified butterfly and the Loop subdivision schemes. Techniques for assigning material properties to geometric subdivision surfaces are derived, and a motion equation for the dynamic model has been formulated using Lagrangian dynamics. Furthermore, advantages of the physics-based deformable models are incorporated into the conventional subdivision schemes, and a dynamic hierarchical control of this model is introduced. Finally, a multiresolution representation of the control mesh is developed and a unified approach for deriving subdivision surface-based finite elements is presented.

The proposed dynamic framework enhances the applicability of the subdivision surfaces in modeling applications. It is also useful for hierarchical shape recovery from large range and volume data sets, as well as for non-rigid motion tracking from a temporal sequence of data sets. Multiresolution representation of the initial mesh controlling the smooth limit surface enables global and local editing of the shape as desired by the modeler. This dynamic framework has also been used for synthesizing

natural terrain models from sparse elevation data.

CHAPTER 1
INTRODUCTION

Generating smooth surfaces of arbitrary topology poses a grand challenge for the computer graphics, computer-aided geometric design and scientific visualization researchers. The existing techniques for modeling smooth complex shapes can be broadly classified into two distinct categories namely, (1) explicit patching using parametric surfaces and (2) subdivision surfaces.

The explicit patching technique involves partitioning the model surface into a collection of individual parametric surface patches. Adjacent surface patches are then explicitly stitched together using continuity constraints. This explicit stitching process is very complicated for modeling smooth surfaces of arbitrary topology due to the continuity constraints which need to be satisfied along the patch boundaries.

Subdivision surfaces are simple procedural models which offer an alternate representation for the smooth surfaces of arbitrary topology. A typical recursive subdivision scheme produces a visually pleasing smooth surface in the limit by repeated application of a fixed set of refinement rules on an user-defined initial control mesh. The initial control mesh is a simple polygonal mesh of the same topological type as that of the smooth surface to be modeled. At each step of subdivision, a *finer* polygonal mesh with more vertices and faces is constructed from the previous one via

1

the refinement process, and the smooth surface is obtained in the limit. However, a few subdivision steps on the initial mesh generally suffice to approximate the smooth surface for all practical purposes. Various sets of rules lead to different subdivision schemes which mainly differ in the smoothness property of the resulting limit surface and/or the type of initial mesh (i.e. triangular, quadrilateral etc.) chosen.

1.1 Problem Statement

To model a smooth surface of arbitrary topology using subdivision surfaces, first a polygonal mesh of same topology needs to be chosen as the initial mesh. This initial mesh, also known as the control mesh, is refined via recursive subdivision using a fixed set of rules, and a smooth surface of the desired topology is obtained in the limit. However, users have to carefully select the initial mesh and/or manipulate the control vertex positions at different levels of subdivision hierarchy in order to satisfy the functional and aesthetic requirements on the smooth limit surface. For example, to obtain a desired effect on the smooth limit surface, it might be necessary to reposition a handful of vertices in the mesh obtained after one subdivision step, or a large number of vertices might need to be moved in the mesh produced after three subdivision steps! This process is not intuitive and at best laborious. Despite the presence of a variety of subdivision schemes in the computer graphics and geometric modeling literature, there is no direct and natural way of manipulating the limit surface. The current state-of-the-art only permits the modeler to interactively obtain the desired effects on the smooth surface by kinematically manipulating the vertex positions at various levels of the subdivision hierarchy. In this dissertation, the challenging problem of directly manipulating the smooth limit surface at arbitrary locations/areas is addressed and a novel solution is presented where the modeler can not only manipulate the smooth limit surface directly but also control the extent of the manipulation effect (i.e., global or local manipulation) on the limit surface.

Subdivision surfaces have also been used for recovering shapes from a given set of points in 3D. However, most of the existing subdivision surface-based shape recovery techniques resort to complex algorithms to derive a mesh for the underlying shape, and then mesh optimization techniques are used to obtain a compact representation of the same. Nevertheless, this process yields a control mesh of the smooth subdivision surface representing the underlying shape that typically uses a large number of degrees of freedom (control vertices) for representation. In this dissertation, an efficient hierarchical method of recovering shapes from range and volume data sets is proposed where the control mesh of the smooth limit surface will use very few degrees of freedom for representation.

1.2 Proposed Solution

Physics-based modeling techniques offer a potential solution to the problem of directly manipulating the smooth limit surface generated by the recursive subdivision procedure. In the physics-based modeling paradigm, a deformable model is derived by assigning mass, damping, stiffness and other physical properties to a surface model. The model is deformed by applying synthesized forces and this deformation is governed by physical laws. Now, if the purely geometric subdivision surface models can be embedded in a physics-based modeling paradigm, then the smooth limit surface can be deformed directly by using physics-based "force" tools. However, this procedure-based surface model obtained through the subdivision process does not have a closed-form analytic formulation in general, and hence poses challenging problems to incorporate mass and damping distribution functions, internal deformation energy, forces, and other physical quantities required to develop a physics-based model. Techniques of locally parameterizing the smooth limit surface generated by various subdivision schemes are proposed in this dissertation. Once a suitable local parameterization scheme is developed for a specific subdivision scheme, a dynamic framework is provided for the corresponding subdivision scheme where the modeler can directly manipulate the smooth limit surface by using synthesized forces. At the same time, a dynamic framework for the wavelets derived using subdivision schemes will assist in adopting a multiresolution representation of the control mesh defining the smooth limit surface, and the modeler can control the extent of manipulation effect by choosing a desired level of editing. Synthesized force application at a lower resolution will yield a global effect whereas manipulations at a finer resolution will have localized effects on the limit surface. The motion of this physics-based deformable subdivision surface model is governed by a second-order differential equation, which is solved numerically using the finite element method. New types of finite elements for the chosen subdivision scheme are also presented for representing the smooth limit surface.

The proposed dynamic framework for the subdivision surfaces provides an efficient solution to the shape recovery problem as well. A simple subdivision surface model with very few vertices in the control mesh can be initialized (positioned) fully inside a given set of points in 3D. The initialized model will be deformed by applying forces synthesized from the given data points. When an equilibrium is obtained, the number of vertices in the control mesh can be increased via a subdivision step on the current control mesh thereby increasing the degrees of freedom for model representation, and a new equilibrium with a better fit to the given data set can be obtained. This process can be repeated till a prescribed error in fit is achieved. Similar approach can be taken for shape recovery from volume data sets as well where a different type of synthesized force needs to be specified. The hierarchical shape recovery process ensures a compact representation of the recovered smooth limit surface using very few degrees of freedom.

1.3   Contributions

In this dissertation, techniques from physics-based modeling are integrated with geometric subdivision methodology to present a scheme for directly manipulating the smooth limit surface generated by the subdivision process. As a result, unlike the existing geometric solutions that only allow the operations on control vertices, the proposed methodology and algorithms permit the user to physically modify the shape of subdivision surfaces at desired locations via application of forces. This gives the user a "virtual" clay/play-dough modeling environment. The proposed model can be edited directly in a hierarchical fashion using synthesized forces. Also, this physics-based subdivision surface model efficiently recovers shapes as well as non-rigid motions from large range and volumetric data sets. Note that this dissertation neither proposes a new subdivision technique nor provides a different interpretation of any existing subdivision technique, but *integrates* the advantages of subdivision surface-based and physics-based modeling techniques to solve important theoretical and practical problems. Although the principles of physics-based modeling are well understood by the graphics experts and modeling researchers, this dissertation will greatly advance the state of the art in physics-based shape modeling due to the contributions listed below.

- Local parameterization techniques for the smooth limit surface generated by various subdivision schemes are systematically derived in a hierarchical framework, and subsequently the initial control polyhedron can be viewed as the parametric domain of the physics-based smooth limit surface.

- The smooth dynamic subdivision surface in the limit is treated as a "real" physical object represented by a set of novel finite elements. The basis (shape) functions of these new variety of finite elements are derived using the subdivision schemes. The proposed finite element methods will prove to be useful not only in the areas of computer graphics and geometric design, but also in engineering analysis as well.

- The subdivision techniques are used to create a surface model that incorporates mass and damping distribution functions, internal deformation energy, forces, and other physical quantities. The motion equations are also systematically derived for this dynamic subdivision surface model whose degrees of freedom are the collection of initial user-specified control vertices. Therefore, the advantages of both the physics-based modeling philosophy and the geometric subdivision schemes are incorporated within a single unified framework.

- Users will be able to manipulate this physics-based model in an arbitrary region, and the model will respond naturally (just like a real-world object would) to this force application. This shape deformation is quantitatively characterized by the time-varying displacement of control points that uniquely define the geometry of the limit surface.

- The dynamic framework for wavelets derived using subdivision schemes enables a multiresolution representation of the control mesh defining the smooth limit surface. This provides additional flexibility to the physics-based modeling framework since the modeler is free to choose the desired editing level. If a lower resolution editing level is chosen, the synthesized force application on the smooth limit surface will have global effects, whereas editing with force-based tools at a finer resolution will yield a localized effect.

- Algorithms and procedures are developed which approximate the proposed new finite elements using a collection of linear and/or bilinear finite elements subject to the implicit geometric constraints enforced by the subdivision rules. This hierarchically-structured approximation can satisfy any user-specified error tolerance.

The proposed dynamic framework enhances the applicability of subdivision surface models in various application areas. It provides a direct and intuitive way of manipulating shapes in a hierarchical fashion for geometric modeling applications. It has also been successfully used for efficient and hierarchical shape recovery from range and volume data sets as well as for tracking a shape of interest from a time sequence of range or volume data sets. Finally, the dynamic framework of subdivision surfaces is combined with a variant of a fractal surface synthesis technique to present a novel natural terrain modeling method.

1.4   Outline of Dissertation

The rest of the dissertation is organized as follows :

Chapter 2 contains an overview of the subdivision surfaces along with a review of the related literature. The motivation for embedding the subdivision surface models in a physics-based modeling framework is discussed, and the proposed model is compared with the existing physics-based models. The advantages of a unified framework for shape modeling and shape recovery are also pointed out in this chapter.

Chapter 3 provides a dynamic framework for the Catmull-Clark subdivision scheme, which is one of the most popular subdivision techniques for modeling complicated objects of arbitrary genus. Analytic formulation of the limit surface generated by the Catmull-Clark subdivision scheme is derived and the "physical" quantities required to develop the dynamic model are introduced [57, 60, 76]. The governing dynamic differential equation is derived using Lagrangian mechanics and is implemented using a finite element technique.

In Chapter 4, a dynamic framework is provided for the butterfly subdivision scheme, another popular subdivision technique for modeling smooth surfaces of arbitrary topology. A local parameterization scheme for the butterfly subdivision surface is derived in a hierarchical style. The physics-based butterfly subdivision model is formulated as a set of novel finite elements which are optimally approximated by a collection of standard finite elements subjected to implicit geometric constraints [58, 61].

Chapter 5 presents an unified approach for providing a dynamic framework for subdivision surfaces in general. In particular, it has been shown that the limit surface obtained using any subdivision scheme can be viewed as a collection of either quadrilateral or triangular finite elements whose basis (shape) functions can be derived using the chosen subdivision scheme [59].

In Chapter 6, a dynamic framework is presented for the subdivision surface-based wavelet schemes. This dynamic framework enables a multiresolution representation of the control mesh defining the smooth limit surface and consequently, the modeler can control the extent of the effect of manipulation on the limit surface by choosing a proper editing level.

In Chapter 7, a system that integrates the implementation of the concepts proposed in earlier chapters is presented. Several modules comprise the entire system, and the functionality of these modules are discussed in this chapter.

The proposed modeling framework is used in various application areas and the results are presented in Chapter 8. The proposed dynamic model has been successfully used in geometric modeling, shape recovery and non-rigid motion estimation applications. A novel technique for natural terrain modeling is also presented where the dynamic framework is combined with a variant of a fractal surface synthesis technique.

Finally, conclusions are drawn in Chapter 9 where future directions of research are also pointed out.

CHAPTER 2
BACKGROUND

In this chapter, a brief overview of the subdivision surfaces is presented followed by a review of the previous work done in the area of subdivision surfaces. This is followed by an overview of the physics-based models along with a review of the related literature. The motivating factors for embedding geometric subdivision surface models in a physics-based modeling paradigm are presented in the next section. The advantages of the proposed dynamic models over the existing physics-based models for shape recovery are discussed and finally advantages of a unified framework for shape modeling and shape recovery are also presented.

2.1 Subdivision Surfaces

The input to any subdivision scheme is an initial mesh (also known as control mesh), $M^0 = (V^0, F^0)$, which is a collection of vertices V^0 and a collection of faces F^0. The subdivision surface $S(M^0)$ associated with the initial mesh M^0 is defined as the limit of the recursive application of the refinement R as shown in Fig.2.1. The refinement R, when applied on a mesh $M^k = (V^k, F^k)$, creates a refined mesh $M^{k+1} = (V^{k+1}, F^{k+1})$ where the vertices in V^{k+1} are computed as affine combinations of the vertices in V^k and the faces in F^{k+1} are obtained by splitting each face in F^k into a fixed number of sub-faces.

11

12

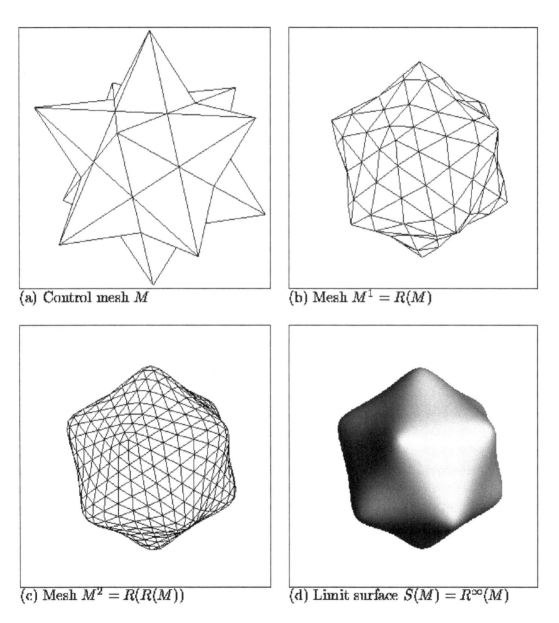

(a) Control mesh M (b) Mesh $M^1 = R(M)$

(c) Mesh $M^2 = R(R(M))$ (d) Limit surface $S(M) = R^\infty(M)$

Figure 2.1. Refinement of an initial control mesh to obtain the limit surface. (Courtesy : H. Hoppe)

It may be noted that the vertices introduced through the subdivision process have a fixed degree in general (4 in case of quadrilateral meshes and 6 in case of triangular meshes). The vertices which do not have this degree are called *extraordinary* vertices. The number of extraordinary vertices are very few as these vertices are not introduced via subdivision refinement in general. For example, in the Catmull-Clark subdivision scheme (defined on quadrilateral meshes) the number of extraordinary vertices does not change after the first subdivision on the initial mesh, whereas in the modified butterfly subdivision scheme (defined on triangular meshes) the subdivision process never introduces an extraordinary vertex. The limit surface defined by the subdivision process is most often C^1(first derivative continuous) or C^2 (second derivative continuous) depending on the subdivision rules expect at very few *extraordinary* points corresponding to the extraordinary vertices in the mesh. Specific subdivision schemes along with the properties of their limit surfaces will be discussed in later chapters.

A lot of research have been carried out on subdivision surfaces, which are mainly focused either on the development of a new subdivision technique or on analyzing the smoothness properties of the limit surface generated by a subdivision scheme. However, in this dissertation the focus is entirely different, namely, embedding the subdivision surfaces in a physics-based modeling paradigm to enhance the applicability of these surface models. In the rest of this section, these "traditional" techniques of subdivision surfaces are reviewed.

Chaikin [14] first introduced the concept of subdivision to the computer graphics community for generating a smooth curve from a given control polygon. During the last two decades, a wide variety of subdivision schemes for modeling smooth surfaces of arbitrary topology have been derived following Chaikin's pioneering work on curve generation. In general, these subdivision schemes can be categorized into two distinct classes namely, (1) approximating subdivision techniques and (2) interpolatory subdivision techniques. The limit surface obtained using an approximating subdivision technique only approximates the initial mesh, whereas the limit surface interpolates the initial mesh in case of interpolatory subdivision techniques.

Among the approximating schemes, the techniques of Doo and Sabin [27, 83] generalize the idea of obtaining uniform biquadratic patches from a rectangular control mesh. This scheme is an example of *vertex subdivision scheme* where a vertex surrounded by k faces is split into k sub-vertices, one for each face. Doo and Sabin's subdivision technique can be applied to any mesh of arbitrary topology, and the resulting smooth limit surface would be biquadratic B-splines, except at extraordinary points corresponding to the extraordinary vertices in the control mesh.

Catmull and Clark [10] developed a method for recursively generating a smooth surface from a polyhedral mesh of arbitrary topology. The Catmull-Clark subdivision surface, defined by an arbitrary initial mesh, can be reduced to a set of standard bicubic B-spline patches except at a finite number of degenerate points. This scheme is an example of *face subdivision scheme*, where a k-sided face is split into k sub-faces. The details of this subdivision scheme are discussed in Section 3.1. Halstead et al. [38] proposed an algorithm to construct a Catmull-Clark subdivision surface that interpolates the vertices of a mesh of arbitrary topology.

Loop [51] presented a subdivision scheme based on the generalization of quartic triangular B-splines for triangular meshes. Loop's subdivision rules are presented in Section 5.3. Hoppe et al. [40] extended Loop's work to produce piecewise smooth surfaces with discontinuities in selected areas of the limit surface. They introduced new subdivision rules that allow for sharp features such as creases and corners in the limit surface.

Peters and Reif [73] proposed a simple subdivision scheme for smoothing polyhedra. Their refinement rules yield a C^1 surface that has a piecewise quadratic parameterization except at isolated extraordinary points. Most recently, non-uniform Doo-Sabin and Catmull-Clark surfaces that generalize non-uniform tensor product B-spline surfaces to arbitrary topologies were introduced by Sederberg et al. [88]. All the schemes mentioned above generalize recursive subdivision schemes for generating limit surfaces with a known parameterization. Various issues involved with character animation using these approximating subdivision schemes were discussed at length by DeRose et al. [25].

The most well-known interpolation-based subdivision scheme is the "butterfly" algorithm proposed by Dyn et al. [30]. Butterfly subdivision method, like other subdivision schemes, makes use of a small number of neighboring vertices for subdivision. It requires simple data structures and is extremely easy to implement. However, it needs a topologically regular setting of the initial (control) mesh in order to obtain a smooth C^1 limit surface. A variant of this scheme with better smoothness properties can be found in Dyn et al. [29]. Zorin et al. [109] developed an improved interpolatory subdivision scheme (which we call the *modified* butterfly scheme) that retains the simplicity of the butterfly scheme and results in much smoother surfaces even from irregular initial meshes. These interpolatory subdivision schemes have extensive applications in wavelets on manifolds, multiresolution decomposition of polyhedral surfaces and multiresolution editing.

A variational approach for interpolatory refinement has been proposed by Kobbelt [43, 44] and by Kobbelt and Schröder [46]. In this approach, the vertex positions in the refined mesh at each subdivision step are obtained by solving an optimization problem. Therefore, these schemes are global, i.e., every new vertex position depends on all the vertex positions of the coarser level mesh. The local refinement property which makes the subdivision schemes attractive for implementation in the computer graphics applications is not retained in the variational approach.

The derivation of various mathematical properties of the smooth limit surface generated by the subdivision algorithms is rather complex. Doo and Sabin [28] first analyzed the smoothness behavior of the limit surface using the Fourier transform and an eigen-analysis of the subdivision matrix. Ball and Storry [3, 4] and Reif [80] further extended Doo and Sabin's prior work on continuity properties of subdivision surfaces by deriving various necessary and sufficient conditions on smoothness for different subdivision schemes. Specific subdivision schemes were analyzed by Schweitzer [87], Habib and Warren [37], Peters and Reif [74] and Zorin [108]. Most recently, Stam

[90] presented a method for exact evaluation of Catmull-Clark subdivision surfaces at arbitrary parameter values. It may be noted that the focus of this dissertation is not on deriving a new subdivision technique or analyzing a subdivision technique, but on deriving a deformable surface model using these subdivision schemes.

2.2   Physics-based Deformable Surface Models

Shape models can be broadly categorized into two types – lumped parameter models and distributed parameter models. A lumped parameter model uses small number of parameters to represent model geometry, whereas a distributed parameter model uses large number of degrees of freedom for model representation. An example of a lumped parameter surface model is a superquadric. Spline surfaces serve as a good example for distributed parameter model.

Deformable surfaces are distributed parameter models which use large number of degrees of freedom for representing the model geometry. A large variety of shapes can be modeled using this type of model, but handling a large number of degrees of freedom can be cumbersome. However, the large degrees of freedom of a deformable model are embedded in a physics-based framework to allow only a "physically mean-ingful" model behavior. Various types of energies are assigned to the model using the degrees of freedom, and the model "deforms" to find an equilibrium state with min-imal energy. The motion equation is derived using Lagrangian dynamics [36], where various energies associated with model gives rise to internal and external forces. The equilibrium state of the model is a model position where the internal deformation force becomes equal to the externally applied force. These physics-based deformable models are useful for modeling where the modeler can deform a surface by applying synthesized forces, and for data fitting where external forces are synthesized from a given data set such that the model approximates the given data at equilibrium.

A deformable surface model is typically parameterized over the domain $[0,1]^2$. Let $\mathbf{s}(u, v, \mathbf{p})$ be a deformable surface model, where $0 \le u, v \le 1$ and $\mathbf{p}$ is a collection of the degrees of freedom p_i, $i = 1, 2, \ldots, n$ associated with the model (assuming the model has n degrees of freedom). The degrees of freedom $p_i(t)$ is a set of generalized coordinates which are functions of time and are assembled into the vector $\mathbf{p}$. Let $f_i(t)$ be the generalized force represented by the vector $\mathbf{f}_p$ and acting on p_i. Let T be the kinetic energy, F be the dissipation energy and U be the potential energy of the deformable surface model. Then, the Lagrangian equation of motion for the model can be expressed as

$$\frac{d}{dt}\frac{\partial T}{\partial \dot{p}_i} - \frac{\partial T}{\partial p_i} + \frac{\partial F}{\partial \dot{p}_i} + \frac{\partial U}{\partial p_i} = f_i. \tag{2.1}$$

Let $\mu(u, v)$ be the mass density function of the surface. Then the kinetic energy of the surface is

$$T = \frac{1}{2} \int \int \mu \dot{\mathbf{s}}^T \dot{\mathbf{s}} \, du \, dv = \frac{1}{2} \dot{\mathbf{p}}^T \mathbf{M} \dot{\mathbf{p}}, \tag{2.2}$$

where $\mathbf{M}$ is called the mass matrix. Similarly, let $\gamma(u, v)$ be the damping density function of the surface. Then the dissipation energy is

$$F = \frac{1}{2} \int \int \gamma \dot{\mathbf{s}}^T \dot{\mathbf{s}} \, du \, dv = \frac{1}{2} \dot{\mathbf{p}}^T \mathbf{D} \dot{\mathbf{p}}, \tag{2.3}$$

where $\mathbf{D}$ is called the damping matrix. The potential energy of the model can be defined using the *thin-plate-under-tension* energy model [96], and is given by

$$
\begin{aligned}
U &= \int\int(\alpha_{11}\frac{\partial \mathbf{s}^T}{\partial u}\frac{\partial \mathbf{s}}{\partial u} + \alpha_{22}\frac{\partial \mathbf{s}^T}{\partial v}\frac{\partial \mathbf{s}}{\partial v} + \beta_{11}\frac{\partial^2 \mathbf{s}^T}{\partial^2 u}\frac{\partial^2 \mathbf{s}}{\partial^2 u} \\
&\quad + \beta_{12}\frac{\partial^2 \mathbf{s}^T}{\partial u\partial v}\frac{\partial^2 \mathbf{s}}{\partial u\partial v} + \beta_{22}\frac{\partial^2 \mathbf{s}^T}{\partial^2 v}\frac{\partial^2 \mathbf{s}}{\partial^2 v})du\,dv \quad = \quad \frac{1}{2}\mathbf{p}^T\mathbf{K}\mathbf{p},
\end{aligned} \tag{2.4}
$$

where $\alpha_{ii}(u,v)$ and $\beta_{ij}(u,v)$ are elasticity functions which control tension and rigidity respectively of the deformable surface model, and $\mathbf{K}$ is known as the stiffness matrix. The discretized equation of motion can be derived using the expressions of the kinetic, dissipation and potential energy in Eqn.2.1, which is given by

$$
\mathbf{M}\ddot{\mathbf{p}} + \mathbf{D}\dot{\mathbf{p}} + \mathbf{K}\mathbf{p} = \mathbf{f}_p, \tag{2.5}
$$

where $\mathbf{f}_p$ is the generalized force vector.

The free-form deformable models discussed above were first introduced to computer graphics and visualization in Terzopoulos et al. [99] and further developed by Terzopoulos and Fleischer [97], Pentland and Williams [72], Metaxas and Terzopoulos [65] and Vemuri and Radisavljevic [104]. Celniker and Gossard [11] developed a system for interactive free-form design based on the finite element optimization of energy functionals proposed in Terzopoulos and Fleischer [97]. Bloor and Wilson [8, 9], Celniker and Welch [12] and Welch and Witkin [105] proposed deformable B-spline curves and surfaces which can be designed by imposing the shape criteria via the minimization of the energy functionals subject to hard or soft geometric constraints through Lagrange multipliers or penalty methods. Qin and Terzopoulos [77, 78, 100] developed dynamic NURBS (D-NURBS) which are very sophisticated models suitable for representing a wide variety of free-form as well as standard analytic shapes. The D-NURBS have the advantage of interactive and direct manipulation of NURBS curves and surfaces, resulting in physically meaningful hence intuitively predictable motion and shape variation.

Deformable models are also widely used for shape recovery, segmentation, motion tracking and other computer vision and medical imaging applications. A detailed survey of deformable models used in these techniques can be found in McInerney and Terzopoulos [64] and the references therein. Some specific existing deformable models used for shape recovery and non-rigid motion estimation will be reviewed in Section 2.4.

2.3   Shape Modeling Using Physics-based Subdivision-surface Model

Recursive subdivision surfaces are powerful for representing smooth geometric shapes of arbitrary topology. However, they constitute a purely geometric representation, and furthermore, conventional geometric modeling with subdivision surfaces may be difficult for representing highly complicated objects. For example, modelers are faced with the tedium of indirect shape modification and refinement through time-consuming operations on a large number of (most often irregular) control vertices when using typical subdivision surface-based modeling schemes. Despite the advent of advanced 3D graphics interaction tools, these indirect geometric operations remain non-intuitive and laborious in general. In addition, it may not be enough to obtain

the most "fair" surface that interpolates a set of (ordered or unorganized) data points.
A certain number of local features such as bulges or inflections may be strongly desired while requiring geometric objects to satisfy global smoothness constraints in
geometric modeling and computer graphics applications. In contrast, physics-based
modeling provides a superior approach to shape modeling that can overcome most of
the limitations associated with traditional geometric modeling approaches. Free-form
deformable models governed by the laws of continuum mechanics are of particular
interest in this context. These dynamic models respond to externally applied forces
in a very intuitive manner. The dynamic formulation marries the model geometry
with time, mass, damping and constraints via a force balance equation. Dynamic
models produce smooth, natural motions which are easy to control. In addition, they
facilitate interaction – especially direct manipulation of complex geometries. Furthermore, the equilibrium state of the model is characterized by a minimum of the
deformation energy of the model subject to the imposed constraints. The deformation
energy functionals can be formulated to satisfy local and global modeling criteria, and
geometric constraints relevant to shape design can also be imposed. The dynamic
approach subsumes all of the aforementioned modeling capabilities in a formulation
which grounds everything in real-world physical behavior.

A severe limitation of the existing deformable models, including D-NURBS, is
that they are defined on a rectangular parametric domain. Hence, it can be very
difficult to model surfaces of arbitrary genus using these models. In a recent work,

DeRose et al. [25] assigned material properties to control meshes at various subdivision levels in order to simulate cloth dynamics using subdivision surfaces. Note that, they assign physical properties on the control meshes at various levels of subdivision and not on the limit surface itself, and hence can not solve the modeling goal we are trying to achieve. In this dissertation, a dynamic framework is presented for subdivision surfaces which combines the benefits of subdivision surfaces for modeling arbitrary topology as well as that of dynamic splines for interactive shape manipulation by applying synthesized forces. The proposed dynamic framework presents the modeler a formal mechanism of direct and intuitive manipulation of the smooth limit surface, as if they were seamlessly sculpting a piece of real-world "clay." A dynamic framework for subdivision surface-based wavelets adds flexibility in the proposed modeling paradigm. It enables a multiresolution representation of the evolving control mesh defining the smooth limit surface, and the modeler can control the extent of manipulation effect by choosing a proper editing level. The formulation and implementation details of these dynamic frameworks are discussed in subsequent chapters.

2.4   Shape and Motion Estimation Using Physics-based Subdivision-surface Model

The dynamic subdivision surface model has been developed primarily for modeling arbitrary (known) topology where modelers can directly manipulate the limit surface by applying synthesized forces in an intuitive fashion. However, another important application of the dynamic subdivision surfaces is in non-rigid shape and motion reconstruction/recovery. Accurate shape recovery requires distributed parameter models which typically possess a large number of degrees of freedom. On the other hand, efficient shape representation imposes the requirement of geometry compression, i.e., models with fewer degrees of freedom. These requirements are conflicting and numerous researchers have been seeking to strike a balance between these contradicting requirements [5, 21, 47, 49, 62, 89, 100, 104]. Another important criterion in the design of shape models is that the initialization of the model during the shape recovery process should not be restricted to globally parameterized input meshes since it may be infeasible to globally parameterize shapes of arbitrary topology. A physics-based model best satisfying the above mentioned criteria is an ideal candidate for a solution to the shape recovery problem for obvious reasons.

Deformable models which come in many varieties, have been used to solve this problem in the physics-based modeling paradigm. These models involve the use of either fixed size [21, 66, 71, 98, 104] or adaptive size [15, 41, 47, 62, 95, 101] grids. The models with fixed grid size generally use less number of degrees of freedom for representation at the cost of accuracy of the recovered shape. On the other hand, models using adaptive grids generally need large number of degrees of freedom to recover the shapes accurately. Note that the shapes being recovered from the image data are smooth in most of the medical applications, i.e. the anatomical structures even with considerable amount of details have more or less a C^1 surface. Under these circumstances, the finite element approaches as in Cohen and Cohen [21] and McInerney and Terzopoulos [62] need a *large* number of degrees of freedom for deriving

24

a smooth and accurate representation. In addition, they can not represent shapes with known arbitrary topology. Moreover, almost all of these schemes require a globally parameterized mesh as their input which may be infeasible at times.

The proposed model solves the shape recovery problem very effectively as it can recover shapes from large range and volume data sets using very few degrees of freedom (control vertices) for its representation and can cope with any arbitrary input mesh, not necessarily parameterized. The initialized model deforms under the influence of synthesized forces to fit the data set by minimizing its energy. Once the approximate shape is recovered, the model is further subdivided automatically and a better approximation to the input data set is achieved using more degrees of freedom. The process of subdivision after achieving an approximate fit is continued till a prescribed error criteria for fitting the data points is achieved. The proposed dynamic subdivision surface models have also been successfully used in motion tracking and visualization of a dynamically deforming shape from a time sequence of volumetric data sets.

2.5 Unified Framework for Shape Recovery and Shape Modeling

Currently, shape recovery and shape modeling are viewed as two distinct areas in computer graphics and geometric modeling literature. However, there are potential benefits if these two can be combined in an unified framework. For example, the modeler starts from scratch to build a specific model in a typical geometric modeling scenario. First, a rough shape is modeled and then it is fine-tuned by manipulating control vertex positions to obtain the desired effects. This turns out a cumbersome process in general. On the other hand, shape recovery using state-of-the-art methods yield large polygonal meshes which are very difficult to manipulate, especially for global changes in shape. Most often the resulting meshes from a shape recovery application are not directly amenable to multiresolution analysis. Computationally expensive re-meshing techniques are needed to convert these meshes into a specific type of meshes on which multiresolution analysis can be performed. This specific type of mesh is known as mesh with "subdivision-connectivity", implying a topologically equivalent mesh with the same connectivity as of the given mesh can be obtained by recursive subdivision of a very simple known initial mesh.

The proposed dynamic framework combines shape recovery and shape modeling in an unified framework where the modeler can scan in 3D points of a prototype model, recover the shape using the proposed dynamic subdivision surface model, and edit at any desired resolution using physics-based force tools. Thus, the modeler is relieved of the burden of both building an initial model and editing a cumbersome huge polygonal mesh. The shape recovery process starts with a smooth subdivision surface model which has a simple initial mesh. This model is deformed using synthesized forces from the given data points and is automatically refined using some pre-defined error in fit criteria. The initial mesh of the final recovered smooth shape has subdivision connectivity in-built, as it is obtained by subdivision refinement, and therefore no re-meshing is needed for multiresolution analysis. The dynamic framework for subdivision surface-based wavelets makes multiresolution editing using physics-based force tools easy to perform. These advantages of shape modeling and shape recovery

in a unified framework will be further illustrated in later chapters.

CHAPTER 3
DYNAMIC CATMULL-CLARK SUBDIVISION SURFACES

Subdivision surfaces, as mentioned earlier, can be broadly classified into two categories – approximating and interpolatory subdivision schemes. The approximating subdivision schemes typically generalize recursive subdivision techniques for generating limit surfaces with known parameterizations. In this chapter, a dynamic framework will be presented for Catmull-Clark subdivision scheme, a popular approximating subdivision technique. The Catmull-Clark subdivision scheme generalizes the idea of obtaining a bicubic B-spline surface by recursive subdivision of a rectangular initial mesh. Before discussing the dynamic framework, first the Catmull-Clark subdivision scheme is briefly reviewed.

3.1   Overview of the Catmull-Clark Subdivision Scheme

Catmull-Clark subdivision scheme, like any other subdivision scheme, starts with a user-defined mesh of arbitrary topology. It refines the initial mesh by adding new vertices, edges and faces with each step of subdivision following a fixed set of subdivision rules. In the limit, a recursively refined polyhedral mesh will converge to a smooth surface. The subdivision rules are as follows:

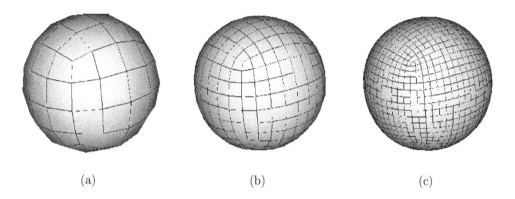

(a)   (b)   (c)

Figure 3.1. Catmull-Clark subdivision : (a) initial mesh, (b) mesh obtained after one step of Catmull-Clark subdivision, and (c) mesh obtained after another subdivision step.

- For each face, a new face vertex is introduced which is the average of all the old vertices defining the face.

- For each (non-boundary) edge, a new edge vertex is introduced which is the average of the following four points: two old vertices defining the edge and two new face vertices of the faces adjacent to the edge.

- For each (non-boundary) vertex V, a new vertex is introduced whose position is $\frac{F}{n} + \frac{2E}{n} + \frac{(n-3)V}{n}$, where F is the average of the new face vertices of all faces adjacent to the old vertex V, E is the average of the midpoints of all the edges incident on the old vertex V and n is the number of the edges incident on the vertex.

- New edges are formed by connecting each new face vertex to the new edge vertices of the edges defining the old face and by connecting each new vertex corresponding to an old vertex to the new edge vertices of all old edges incident on the old vertex.

- New faces are defined as faces enclosed by new edges.

An example of Catmull-Clark subdivision on an initial mesh is shown in Fig.3.1. The most important property of the Catmull-Clark subdivision surfaces is that a smooth surface can be generated from any control mesh of arbitrary topology. There-fore, this subdivision scheme is extremely valuable for modeling various complicated geometric objects of arbitrary topology. Catmull-Clark subdivision surfaces include standard bicubic B-spline surfaces as their special case (i.e., the limit surface is a bicubic B-spline surface for a rectangular mesh with all non-boundary vertices of degree 4). In addition, the aforementioned subdivision rules generalize the recur-sive bicubic B-spline patch subdivision algorithm. For non-rectangular meshes, the limit surface converges to a bicubic B-spline surface except at a finite number of ex-traordinary points. These extraordinary points correspond to extraordinary vertices (vertices whose degree is not equal to 4) in the mesh. Note that, after the first sub-division, all faces are quadrilaterals, hence all the new vertices created subsequently will have four incident edges. The number of extraordinary points on the limit sur-face is a constant, and is equal to the number of extraordinary vertices in the refined mesh obtained after applying one step of the Catmull-Clark subdivision on the initial mesh. The limit surface is curvature-continuous everywhere except at extraordinary vertices, where only tangent plane continuity is achieved. In spite of the popularity of Catmull-Clark subdivision surfaces for representing complex geometric shapes of arbitrary topology, these subdivision surfaces may not be easily parameterizable and deriving a closed-form analytic formulation of the limit surface can be very difficult. These deficiencies preclude their immediate pointwise manipulation and hence may restrain the applicability of these schemes. In the rest of the chapter, a dynamic framework is developed for the Catmull-Clark subdivision surfaces which offers a closed-form analytic formulation and allows users to manipulate the model directly and intuitively. It may be noted that recently a scheme was proposed by Stam [90] for directly evaluating the Catmull-Clark subdivision surfaces at arbitrary parameter values, but the work presented here on dynamic Catmull-Clark subdivision surfaces [57, 60, 76] was published prior to the publication of the above-mentioned work.

3.2 Formulation

In this section, a systematic formulation of the new dynamic model based on Catmull-Clark subdivision surfaces is presented. This dynamic model treats the smooth limit surface as a function of its initial mesh. However, the control vertex positions need to be updated continually at every level of subdivision in order to develop the dynamic framework. Note that, all the vertices introduced through subdivision are obtained as an affine combination of control vertex positions in the initial mesh. Therefore, the dynamic behavior of the limit surface can be controlled by formulating the dynamic model on the initial mesh itself, the only exception being the case when the initial mesh has non-rectangular faces. This problem can be circumvented by taking the mesh obtained through one step of subdivision as the initial mesh. It may be noted that an additional subdivision step may be needed in some cases to isolate the extraordinary points, and the resulting mesh is treated as the initial mesh. A typical example of the above mentioned scenario is when the initial mesh is a tetrahedron where two subdivision steps are needed, and the dynamic framework can be developed by treating the mesh obtained after two subdivision steps as the initial mesh. To define the limit surface using the vertices of the initial mesh, the enumeration of the bicubic patches in the limit surface is necessary. In the next two sections, various schemes are presented for assigning the bicubic patches to various faces of the initial mesh.

3.2.1   Assigning Patches to Regular Faces

In Fig.3.2, a rectangular control mesh is shown along with the bicubic B-spline surface (4 patches) in the limit after an infinite number of subdivision steps. Note that, each of the bicubic patches in the limit surface is defined by a rectangular face with each vertex of degree four, thereby accounting for 16 control points (from its 8 connected neighborhood) needed to define a bicubic surface patch in the limit. Therefore, for each rectangular face in the initial mesh with a degree of 4 at each vertex, the corresponding bicubic surface patch can be assigned to it in a straight forward way. In Fig.3.2, the surface patches S_1, S_2, S_3 and S_4 are assigned to face F_1, F_2, F_3 and F_4 respectively. The 16 control points for the patch S_1, corresponding to face F_1, are highlighted in Fig.3.2. Note that, the initial control mesh can be viewed as the parametric domain of the limit surface. Therefore, face F_1 can be thought of as the portion of the parametric domain over which the patch S_1 is defined, i.e., has non-zero values. Nevertheless, each rectangular face (e.g. F_1) can be parametrically

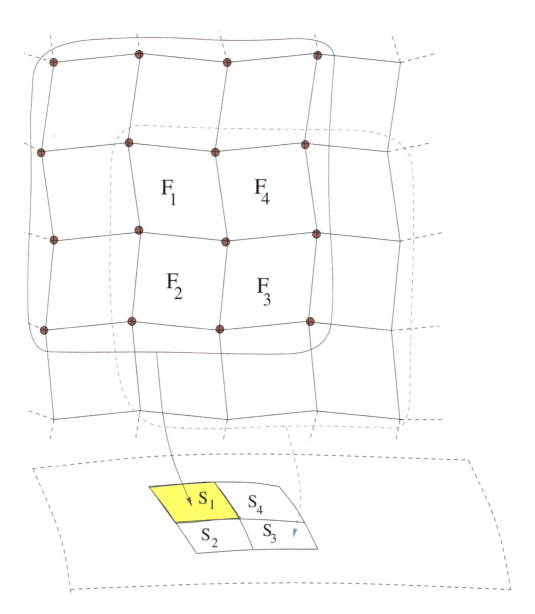

Figure 3.2. A rectangular mesh and its limit surface consisting of 4 bicubic surface patches.

defined over $[0,1]^2$, and hence, all bicubic B-spline patches defined by 16 control points are locally parameterized over $[0,1]^2$.

3.2.2 Assigning Patches to Irregular Faces

In Fig.3.3, a mesh containing an extraordinary point of degree 3 and its limit surface are shown. The faces $F_0, F_1, \ldots, F_8$ are assigned to bicubic patches $S_0, S_1, \ldots, S_8$ respectively (as they all have vertices of degree 4) following the aforementioned scheme. However, the central smooth surface enclosed by the patches $S_0, S_1, \ldots, S_8$ consists of infinite number of bicubic patches converging to a point in the limit. A recursive way of enumerating these bicubic patches and assigning them to various faces at different levels need to be developed in order to formulate the dynamic framework for Catmull-Clark subdivision surface model.

The idea of enumerating the bicubic patches corresponding to faces having an extraordinary vertex is shown in Fig.3.4 where a local subdivision of the mesh consisting of faces $F_0, F_1, ..., F_8, P_0, P_1, P_2$ (and not the other boundary faces) of Fig.3.3 is carried out. Topologically, the resulting local subdivision mesh (shown as dotted mesh) is exactly the same as the mesh in Fig.3.3 and hence exactly the same number of bicubic patches can be assigned to its faces with vertices of degree 4 as is evident from Fig.3.4 (the new faces and the corresponding patches are marked by "p" and "n" respectively). This process of local subdivision and assignment of bicubic patches around an extraordinary point can be carried out recursively and in the limit, the enclosed patch corresponding to faces sharing the extraordinary point will converge to a point. However, there is no need to carry out an infinite number of subdivision

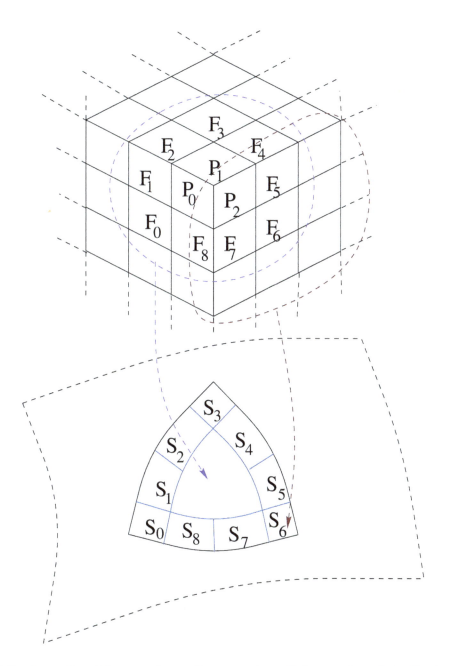

Figure 3.3. A mesh with an extraordinary point of degree 3 and its limit surface.

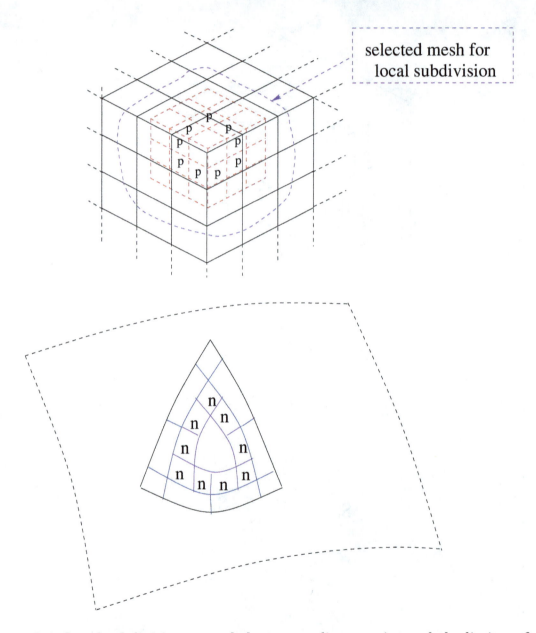

Figure 3.4. Local subdivision around the extraordinary point and the limit surface.

steps. This description is for formulation purposes only and the exact implementation will be detailed in a later section.

3.2.3 Kinematics

In this section, the mathematics for the kinematics of the limit surface is developed via illustrative examples and then the generalized formulas are presented. It may be noted that a single bicubic B-spline patch is obtained as the limiting process of the Catmull-Clark subdivision algorithm applied to an initial 4 by 4 rectangular control mesh. Let $\mathbf{s}_p(u, v)$, where $(u, v) \in [0, 1]^2$, denote this bicubic B-spline patch which can be expressed analytically as

$$\mathbf{s}_p(u, v) = (x(u, v), y(u, v), z(u, v))^T = \sum_{i=0}^{3} \sum_{j=0}^{3} \mathbf{d}_{i,j} B_{i,4}(u) B_{j,4}(v), \qquad (3.1)$$

where $\mathbf{d}_{i,j}$ represents a 3-dimensional position vector at the (i, j)th control point location and $B_{i,4}(u)$ and $B_{j,4}(v)$ are the cubic B-spline basis functions. The subscript p on $\mathbf{s}$ denotes the patch under consideration. Expressing Eqn.3.1 in a generalized coordinate system we have

$$\mathbf{s}_p = \mathbf{J}_p \mathbf{q}_p, \qquad (3.2)$$

where $\mathbf{J}_p$ is a transformation matrix storing the basis functions of a bicubic B-spline patch, and is of size $(3, 48)$. Vector $\mathbf{q}_p$ is the concatenation of all control points defining a B-spline patch in 3D. Note that in the concatenation of the control points, each control point has an (x, y, z) component. For example, the (x, y, z) components of the control point (i, j) correspond to positions $3k, 3k + 1, 3k + 2$ - where, $k =$

$4i + j$ - respectively in the vector $\mathbf{q}_p$. We can express the entries of $\mathbf{J}_p$ explicitly in the following way: $\mathbf{J}_p(0, k) = \mathbf{J}_p(1, k + 1) = \mathbf{J}_p(2, k + 2) = B_{i,4}(u)B_{j,4}(v)$ and $\mathbf{J}_p(0, k + 1) = \mathbf{J}_p(0, k + 2) = \mathbf{J}_p(1, k) = \mathbf{J}_p(1, k + 2) = \mathbf{J}_p(2, k) = \mathbf{J}_p(2, k + 1) = 0$.

Limit surface with many bicubic patches from a rectangular initial mesh

Now a limit surface consisting of many bicubic surface patches obtained after applying an infinite number of subdivision steps to a rectangular initial mesh is considered. For example, let the limit surface of Fig.3.2 be $\mathbf{s}_m$ which can be written as

$$\mathbf{s}_m(u, v) = \mathbf{s}_{m_1}(2u, 2v) + \mathbf{s}_{m_2}(2(u - \frac{1}{2}), 2v) + \mathbf{s}_{m_3}(2(u - \frac{1}{2}), 2(v - \frac{1}{2})) + \mathbf{s}_{m_4}(2u, 2(v - \frac{1}{2})),$$
(3.3)

where $\mathbf{s}_{m_1}(2u, 2v) = \mathbf{s}_m(u, v)$ for $0 \leq u, v \leq \frac{1}{2}$, and 0 otherwise. Similarly, $\mathbf{s}_{m_2}, \mathbf{s}_{m_3}$ and $\mathbf{s}_{m_4}$ are also equal to $s_m(u, v)$ for an appropriate range of values of u, v and 0 outside. It may be noted that $\mathbf{s}_{m_1}, \mathbf{s}_{m_2}, \mathbf{s}_{m_3}, \mathbf{s}_{m_4}$ correspond to patches S_1, S_2, S_3, S_4 respectively in Fig.3.2. Eqn.3.3 in generalized coordinates becomes

$$\mathbf{s}_m = \mathbf{J}_1\mathbf{q}_1 + \mathbf{J}_2\mathbf{q}_2 + \mathbf{J}_3\mathbf{q}_3 + \mathbf{J}_4\mathbf{q}_4 = \sum_{i=1}^{4} \mathbf{J}_i\mathbf{q}_i,$$
(3.4)

where $\mathbf{J}_i$s are the transformation matrices of size $(3, 48)$ and $\mathbf{q}_i$s are the (x,y,z) component concatenation of a subset of the control points of $\mathbf{s}_m$ defining $\mathbf{s}_{m_i}$, $i = 1, 2, 3$

and 4. A more general expression for $\mathbf{s}_m$ is

$$\mathbf{s}_m = \mathbf{J}_1\mathbf{A}_1\mathbf{q}_m + \mathbf{J}_2\mathbf{A}_2\mathbf{q}_m + \mathbf{J}_3\mathbf{A}_3\mathbf{q}_m + \mathbf{J}_4\mathbf{A}_4\mathbf{q}_m = \sum_{i=1}^{4}\mathbf{J}_i\mathbf{A}_i\mathbf{q}_m = \mathbf{J}_m\mathbf{q}_m. \qquad (3.5)$$

Where, $\mathbf{q}_m$ is the 75-component vector of 3D positions of the 25 vertex control mesh defining the limit surface $\mathbf{s}_m$. Matrices $\mathbf{A}_i, 1 \leq i \leq 4$, are of size $(48, 75)$, each row consisting of a single nonzero entry $(= 1)$ and the $(3, 75)$-sized matrix $\mathbf{J}_m = \sum_{i=1}^{4}\mathbf{J}_i\mathbf{A}_i$.

Limit surface with many bicubic patches from an arbitrary initial mesh

The stage is now set to define the limit surface $\mathbf{s}$ using the vertices of initial mesh $\mathcal{M}$ for any arbitrary topology, assuming all faces are quadrilateral and no face contains more than one extraordinary point as its vertex (i.e., extraordinary points are isolated). As mentioned earlier, if these assumptions are not satisfied, one or two steps of global subdivision may be required and the resulting mesh can be treated as the initial mesh. Let the number of vertices in the initial mesh $\mathcal{M}$ be a, and let l of these be the extraordinary vertices. The number of faces in the initial mesh are assumed to be b, and k of these faces have vertices with degree 4 (henceforth termed a "normal face") and each of the remaining $(b-k)$ faces have one of the l extraordinary vertices (henceforth termed a "special face"). Let $\mathbf{p}$ be the $3a = N$ dimensional vector containing the control vertex positions in 3D. Using the formulations in Section 3.2.1

and Section 3.2.2, the smooth limit surface can be expressed as

$$\mathbf{s} = \sum_{i=1}^{k} \mathbf{n}_i + \sum_{j=1}^{l} \mathbf{s}_j, \tag{3.6}$$

where $\mathbf{n}_i$ is a single bicubic patch assigned to each of the normal faces and $\mathbf{s}_j$ is a collection of infinite number of bicubic patches corresponding to each of the extraordinary points. As $\mathbf{s}$ is a surface defined over the faces of the initial control mesh, each $\mathbf{n}_i$ can be viewed as a bicubic patch defined over the corresponding regular face in the initial control mesh. Similarly, each $\mathbf{s}_j$ can be defined over the corresponding irregular faces in the initial mesh (refer to Fig.3.2 – Fig.3.4 for the detailed description on parametric domains of subdivision surfaces). For the simplicity of the following mathematical derivations on the dynamic model, from now on the parametric domain will not be explicitly provided in the formulation. Employing the same approach taken before to derive Eqn.3.5, it can be shown that

$$\sum_{i=1}^{k} \mathbf{n}_i = \sum_{i=1}^{k} (^n\mathbf{J}_i)(^n\mathbf{p}_i) = (\sum_{i=1}^{k} (^n\mathbf{J}_i)(^n\mathbf{A}_i))\mathbf{p} = (^n\mathbf{J})\mathbf{p}, \tag{3.7}$$

where $^n\mathbf{J}_i, ^n\mathbf{p}_i$ and $^n\mathbf{A}_i$ are the equivalent of $\mathbf{J}_i, \mathbf{p}_i$ in Eqn.3.4 and $\mathbf{A}_i$ in Eqn.3.5 respectively. The pre-superscript n is used to indicate that these mathematical quantities describe bicubic patch in the limit surface corresponding to normal faces.

The following **notational convention** will be used for describing various mathematical quantities used in the derivation of the expression for a collection of infinite number of bicubic patches around an extraordinary vertex. The pre-superscript s

is used to represent a collection of bicubic patches around an extraordinary vertex, the subscript j is used to indicate the j-th extraordinary point, the post-superscript represents the exponent of a mathematical quantity and the level indicator (to represent various levels of subdivision in the local control mesh around an extraordinary vertex) is depicted via a subscript on the curly braces.

The expression for $\mathbf{s}_j$ is derived using the recursive nature of local subdivision around an extraordinary vertex as shown in Section 3.2.2. First, $\mathbf{s}_j$ can be expressed as

$$\mathbf{s}_j = \{{}^s\mathbf{J}_j\}_1 \{{}^s\mathbf{p}_j\}_1 + \{\mathbf{s}_j\}_1, \tag{3.8}$$

where the first term of Eqn.3.8 is the generalized coordinate representation of the bicubic B-spline patches corresponding to the normal faces of the new local subdivision mesh obtained after one subdivision step on the local control mesh (similar to those patches marked n in Fig.3.4). $\{\mathbf{s}_j\}_1$ represents the rest of the infinite bicubic B-spline patches surrounding the extraordinary point (similar to the central patch enclosed by patches marked n in Fig.3.4). The vertices in the newly obtained local subdivision mesh $\{{}^s\mathbf{p}_j\}_1$ can be expressed as a linear combination of a subset of the vertices of the initial mesh $\mathcal{M}$ (which will contribute to the local subdivision) following the subdivision rules. We can name this subset of initial control vertices $\{{}^s\mathbf{p}_j\}_0$. Furthermore, there exists a matrix $\{{}^s\mathbf{B}_j\}_1$ of size $(3c, 3d)$, such that $\{{}^s\mathbf{B}_j\}_1 \{{}^s\mathbf{p}_j\}_0 = \{{}^s\mathbf{p}_j\}_1$ where $\{{}^s\mathbf{p}_j\}_1$ and $\{{}^s\mathbf{p}_j\}_0$ are vectors of dimension $3c$ and $3d$ respectively. Applying the idea of recursive local subdivision again on $\{\mathbf{s}_j\}_1$, $\mathbf{s}_j$ can be further expanded as

$$\mathbf{s}_j = \{{}^s\mathbf{J}_j\}_1\{{}^s\mathbf{B}_j\}_1\{{}^s\mathbf{p}_j\}_0 + \{{}^s\mathbf{J}_j\}_2\{{}^s\mathbf{B}_j\}_2\{{}^s\tilde{\mathbf{p}}_j\}_1 + \{\mathbf{s}_j\}_2. \tag{3.9}$$

In the above derivation, $\{{}^s\tilde{\mathbf{p}}_j\}_1$ is a vector of dimension $3d$, comprising of a subset of the vertices defining the $3c$ dimensional vector $\{{}^s\mathbf{p}_j\}_1$. Note that, $\{{}^s\tilde{\mathbf{p}}_j\}_1$ has the same structure as $\{{}^s\mathbf{p}_j\}_0$, therefore, there exists a $(3d, 3d)$ matrix $\{{}^s\mathbf{C}_j\}_1$ such that $\{{}^s\mathbf{C}_j\}_1\{{}^s\mathbf{p}_j\}_0 = \{{}^s\tilde{\mathbf{p}}_j\}_1$. Each subdivision of a local mesh with d vertices creates a new local mesh with c vertices which contributes a fixed number of bicubic B-spline patches. Proceeding one step further, it can be shown that

$$\begin{aligned} \mathbf{s}_j &= \{{}^s\mathbf{J}_j\}_1\{{}^s\mathbf{B}_j\}_1\{{}^s\mathbf{p}_j\}_0 + \{{}^s\mathbf{J}_j\}_2\{{}^s\mathbf{B}_j\}_2\{{}^s\mathbf{C}_j\}_1\{{}^s\mathbf{p}_j\}_0 \\ &\quad + \{{}^s\mathbf{J}_j\}_3\{{}^s\mathbf{B}_j\}_3\{{}^s\mathbf{C}_j\}_1^2\{{}^s\mathbf{p}_j\}_0 + \{\mathbf{s}_j\}_3. \end{aligned} \tag{3.10}$$

Because of the intrinsic property of the local recursive subdivision around the extraordinary point, we have $\{{}^s\mathbf{J}_j\}_1 = \{{}^s\mathbf{J}_j\}_2 = \ldots = \{{}^s\mathbf{J}_j\}_n = \ldots = \{{}^s\mathbf{J}_j\}_\infty$. In addition, the subdivision rules remain the same throughout the refinement process, we also have $\{{}^s\mathbf{B}_j\}_1 = \{{}^s\mathbf{B}_j\}_2 = \ldots = \{{}^s\mathbf{B}_j\}_n = \ldots = \{{}^s\mathbf{B}_j\}_\infty$. So, the above equations can be further simplified leading to

$$\begin{aligned} \mathbf{s}_j &= \{{}^s\mathbf{J}_j\}_1\{{}^s\mathbf{B}_j\}_1\{{}^s\mathbf{p}_j\}_0 + \{{}^s\mathbf{J}_j\}_1\{{}^s\mathbf{B}_j\}_1\{{}^s\mathbf{C}_j\}_1\{{}^s\mathbf{p}_j\}_0 \\ &\quad + \{{}^s\mathbf{J}_j\}_1\{{}^s\mathbf{B}_j\}_1\{{}^s\mathbf{C}_j\}_1^2\{{}^s\mathbf{p}_j\}_0 + \cdots \\ &= \{{}^s\mathbf{J}_j\}_1\{{}^s\mathbf{B}_j\}_1\left(\sum_{i=0}^{\infty}\{{}^s\mathbf{C}_j\}_1^i\right)\{{}^s\mathbf{p}_j\}_0. \end{aligned} \tag{3.11}$$

Vector $\mathbf{s}_j$ can be written as

$$\mathbf{s}_j = ({}^s\mathbf{J}_j)({}^s\mathbf{p}_j), \tag{3.12}$$

where ${}^s\mathbf{J}_j = \{{}^s\mathbf{J}_j\}_1\{{}^s\mathbf{B}_j\}_1(\sum_{i=0}^{\infty}\{{}^s\mathbf{C}_j\}_1^i)$ and ${}^s\mathbf{p}_j = \{{}^s\mathbf{p}_j\}_0$. The idea of local recursive subdivision around an extraordinary point is illustrated in Fig.3.5. Note that, each vertex position in the subdivided mesh is obtained by an affine combination of some vertices in the previous level and hence any row of $\{{}^s\mathbf{C}_j\}_1$ sums to 1. The largest eigenvalue of such a matrix is 1 and it can be shown that the corresponding infinite series is convergent following a similar approach as in Halstead et al. [38]. The rest of the derivation leading to an expression for $\mathbf{s}$ is relatively straight forward. Using the same approach used to derive the Eqn.3.7, it can be shown that

$$\sum_{j=1}^{l}\mathbf{s}_j = \sum_{j=1}^{l}({}^s\mathbf{J}_j)({}^s\mathbf{p}_j) = (\sum_{j=1}^{l}({}^s\mathbf{J}_j)({}^s\mathbf{A}_j))\mathbf{p} = ({}^s\mathbf{J})\mathbf{p}. \tag{3.13}$$

From Eqn.3.6, Eqn.3.7 and Eqn.3.13,

$$\mathbf{s} = ({}^n\mathbf{J})\mathbf{p} + ({}^s\mathbf{J})\mathbf{p}. \tag{3.14}$$

Let $\mathbf{J} = ({}^n\mathbf{J}) + ({}^s\mathbf{J})$, and hence

$$\mathbf{s} = \mathbf{J}\mathbf{p}. \tag{3.15}$$

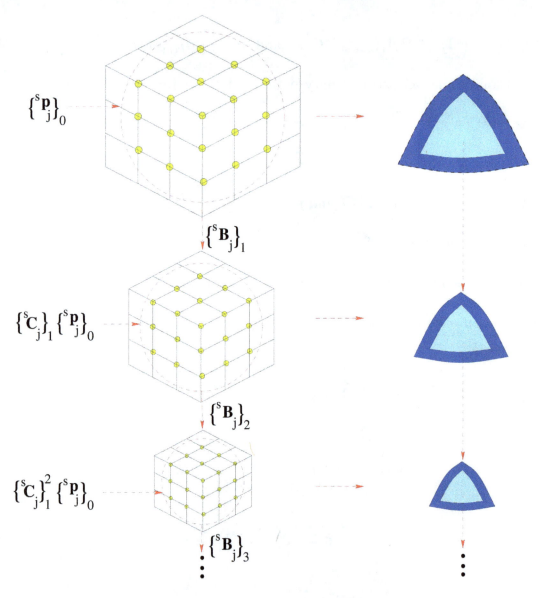

Figure 3.5. Local subdivision around the extraordinary point and the corresponding patches in the limit surface from different levels of subdivision.

3.2.4   Dynamics

In the previous section, an expression is derived for the smooth limit surface obtained via infinite subdivision steps. This expression treats the smooth limit surface as a function of the control vertex positions in the initial mesh. Now the vertex positions in the initial mesh defining the smooth limit surface $\mathbf{s}$ are treated as a function of time in order to embed the Catmull-Clark subdivision model in a dynamic framework. The velocity of this surface model can be expressed as

$$\dot{\mathbf{s}}(u, v, \mathbf{p}) = \mathbf{J}\dot{\mathbf{p}}, \tag{3.16}$$

where an overstruck dot denotes a time derivative. The physics of the dynamic subdivision surface model is based on the work-energy version of Lagrangian dynamics [36] and is formulated in an analogous way to the dynamic framework presented in Section 2.2.

Let $\mu(u, v)$ be the mass density function of the surface. Then the kinetic energy of the surface is

$$T \;=\; \frac{1}{2} \int \int \mu \dot{\mathbf{s}}^T \dot{\mathbf{s}}\, dudv \;=\; \frac{1}{2}\dot{\mathbf{p}}^T \mathbf{M}\dot{\mathbf{p}}, \tag{3.17}$$

where (using Eqn.3.16)

$$\mathbf{M} = \int \int \mu \mathbf{J}^T \mathbf{J}\, dudv \tag{3.18}$$

is the mass matrix of size (N, N). Similarly, let $\gamma(u, v)$ be the damping density function of the surface. Then the dissipation energy is

$$F = \frac{1}{2} \int\int \gamma \dot{\mathbf{s}}^T \dot{\mathbf{s}} du dv = \frac{1}{2} \dot{\mathbf{p}}^T \mathbf{D} \dot{\mathbf{p}}, \tag{3.19}$$

where

$$\mathbf{D} = \int\int \gamma \mathbf{J}^T \mathbf{J} du dv \tag{3.20}$$

is the damping matrix of size (N, N).

The potential energy of the smooth limit surface can be expressed as

$$U = \frac{1}{2} \mathbf{p}^T \mathbf{K} \mathbf{p}, \tag{3.21}$$

where $\mathbf{K}$ is the stiffness matrix of size (N, N). A *thin-plate-under-tension* energy model [96] is used to compute the elastic potential energy of the dynamic subdivision surface. The corresponding expression for the stiffness matrix $\mathbf{K}$ is

$$\mathbf{K} = \int\int (\alpha_{11}\mathbf{J}_u^T\mathbf{J}_u + \alpha_{22}\mathbf{J}_v^T\mathbf{J}_v + \beta_{11}\mathbf{J}_{uu}^T\mathbf{J}_{uu} + \beta_{12}\mathbf{J}_{uv}^T\mathbf{J}_{uv} + \beta_{22}\mathbf{J}_{vv}^T\mathbf{J}_{vv}) du dv. \tag{3.22}$$

where the subscripts on $\mathbf{J}$ denote the parametric partial derivatives. The $\alpha_{ii}(u, v)$ and $\beta_{ij}(u, v)$s are elasticity functions controlling local tension and rigidity in the two parametric coordinate directions. Note that the thin-plate energy expression might diverge at extraordinary points on the limit surface for Catmull-Clark subdivision scheme as shown in Halstead et al. [38]. Several methods have been suggested in

Halstead et al. [38] to overcome the problem of the divergent series. However, in this

dissertation, the problem is circumvented by setting the corresponding rigidity coef-

ficients to be zero at these points. Therefore, the thin-plate energy at extraordinary

points is zero. The effect is negligible to the overall thin-plate energy as *very few*

extraordinary points are present in the smooth limit surface.

Using the expressions for the kinetic, dissipation and potential energy in Eqn.2.1,

the same motion equation as in Eqn.2.5 can be obtained. The generalized force vector

$\mathbf{f}_p$, which can be obtained through the principle of virtual work [36], is expressed as

$$\mathbf{f}_p = \int \int \mathbf{J}^T \mathbf{f}(u, v, t) du dv \tag{3.23}$$

Different types of forces can be applied on the smooth limit surface, and the limit

surface would evolve over time according to Eqn.2.5 to obtain an equilibrium position

characterized by a minimum of the total model energy.

3.2.5 Multilevel Dynamics

At this point, a dynamic framework is developed for the Catmull-Clark subdi-

vision scheme where the smooth limit surface evolves over time in response to the

applied forces. The entire process can be described as follows. Given an initial mesh,

a smooth surface is obtained in the limit. Users can directly apply synthesized forces

to this smooth limit surface to enforce various functional and aesthetic constraints.

This direct manipulation is then transferred back as virtual forces acting on the initial

mesh through a transformation matrix (Eqn.3.23), and the initial mesh (as well as

the underlying smooth limit surface) deforms continuously over time until an equilibrium position is obtained. The deformation of the surface in response to the applied
forces is governed by the motion equation (Eqn.2.5). Within the physics-based modeling framework, the limit surface evolves as a consequence of the evolution of the
initial mesh. One can apply various types of forces on the limit surface to obtain
a desired effect, but the possible level of details appearing in a shape that can be
obtained through evolution is constrained by the number of control vertices in the
initial mesh. It might be necessary to increase the number of control vertices in the
initial mesh in order to obtain a detailed shape through this evolution process.

The number of control vertices defining the same smooth limit surface can be
increased by simply replacing the initial mesh with a mesh obtained after one subdivision step applied to the initial mesh. This new mesh has more number of vertices
but defines the same limit surface. Therefore, the dynamic Catmull-Clark surface
model can be subdivided globally to increase the number of vertices (control points)
of the model. For example, after one step of global subdivision, the initial degrees of
freedom $\mathbf{p}$ (refer to Eqn.3.15 and Eqn.3.16) in the dynamic system will be replaced
by a larger number of degrees of freedom $\mathbf{q}$, where $\mathbf{q} = \mathbf{A}\mathbf{p}$. $\mathbf{A}$ is a global subdivision matrix of size (M, N) whose entries are uniquely determined by Catmull-Clark
subdivision rules (see Section 3.1 for the details about the rules). Thus, $\mathbf{p}$, expressed
as a function of $\mathbf{q}$, can be written as

$$\mathbf{p} = \left(\mathbf{A}^T\mathbf{A}\right)^{-1}\mathbf{A}^T\mathbf{q} = \mathbf{A}^\dagger\mathbf{q}, \tag{3.24}$$

where $\mathbf{A}^\dagger = (\mathbf{A}^T\mathbf{A})^{-1}\mathbf{A}^T$. Therefore, Eqn.3.15 and Eqn.3.16 can be rewritten as

$$\mathbf{s} = (\mathbf{J}\mathbf{A}^\dagger)\mathbf{q}, \qquad (3.25)$$

and

$$\dot{\mathbf{s}}(u, v, \mathbf{q}) = (\mathbf{J}\mathbf{A}^\dagger)\dot{\mathbf{q}}, \qquad (3.26)$$

respectively. Now the equation of motion needs to be derived for this new subdivided model involving a larger number of control vertices namely $\mathbf{q}$. The mass, damping and stiffness matrices need to be recomputed for this "finer" level. The structure of the motion equation as given by Eqn.2.5 remains unchanged, but the dimensionality and the entries of $\mathbf{M}, \mathbf{D}, \mathbf{K}, \mathbf{p}$ and $\mathbf{f}_p$ change correspondingly in this newly obtained subdivided level. In particular the motion equation, explicitly expressed as a function of $\mathbf{q}$, can be written as

$$\mathbf{M}_q\ddot{\mathbf{q}} + \mathbf{D}_q\dot{\mathbf{q}} + \mathbf{K}_q\mathbf{q} = \mathbf{f}_q, \qquad (3.27)$$

where $\mathbf{M}_q = \int\int \mu(\mathbf{A}^\dagger)^T\mathbf{J}^T\mathbf{J}\mathbf{A}^\dagger dudv$ and the derivation of $\mathbf{D}_q, \mathbf{K}_q$ and $\mathbf{f}_q$ follow suit.

It may be noted that further subdivision, if necessary, can be carried out in a similar fashion. Therefore, multilevel dynamics is achieved through recursive subdivision on the initial set of control vertices. Users can interactively choose the level of detail representation of the dynamic model as appropriate for their modeling and design requirements. Alternatively, the system can automatically determine the level of subdivision most suitable for an application depending on some application-specific criteria.

3.3   Finite Element Implementation

The evolution of the generalized coordinates for our new dynamic surface model can be determined by the second-order differential equation as given by Eqn.2.5. An analytical solution of the governing differential equation can not be derived in general. However, an efficient numerical implementation can be obtained using the finite element method [42]. The limit surface of the dynamic Catmull-Clark subdivision model is a collection of bicubic patch elements. We use two types of finite elements for this purpose - normal elements (bicubic patches assigned to the normal faces of the initial mesh) and special elements (collection of infinite number of bicubic patches assigned to each extraordinary vertex of the initial mesh). The shape functions for the normal element are the basis functions of the bicubic surface patch, whereas the shape functions for the special element are the collection of basis functions corresponding to the bicubic patches in the special element. In the current implementation, the $\mathbf{M}$, $\mathbf{D}$ and $\mathbf{K}$ matrices for each individual normal and special elements are calculated and they can be assembled into the global $\mathbf{M}$, $\mathbf{D}$ and $\mathbf{K}$ matrices that appear in the corresponding discrete equation of motion. In practice, we never assemble the global matrices explicitly in the interest of time performance. The detailed implementation is explained in the following sections.

3.3.1   Data Structures

The limit surface of the dynamic Catmull-Clark subdivision model is a collection of bicubic patches, and hence requires us to keep track of the control polygons defining such patches. We can get the control polygons for the normal elements in the limit

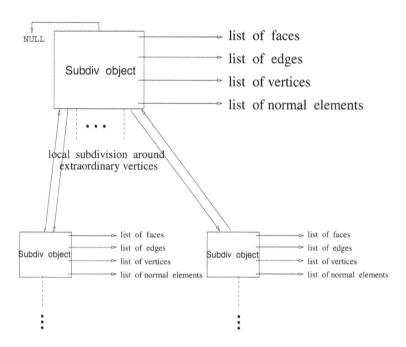

Figure 3.6. The data structure used for dynamic subdivision surface implementation.

surface from the initial control mesh itself. However, we need to locally subdivide the initial control mesh around the extraordinary vertices to obtain the control polygons of the bicubic patches in the special elements on the limit surface.

A subdivision surface defined by a control mesh at any level is designed as a class which has a pointer to its parent mesh, a set of pointers to its offspring meshes (arising out of local subdivision around the extraordinary vertices at that level), a list of faces, edges, vertices and normal elements . Face, edge, vertex and normal elements are, in turn, classes which store all the connectivity and other information needed to either enumerate all the patches or locally subdivide around an extraordinary vertex in that level. The implementation takes the initial mesh as the base subdivision surface object (with its parent pointer set to NULL) and locally subdivides the initial mesh upto a user-defined maximum level around each extraordinary vertex to create offspring objects at different levels (Fig.3.6). At this point, let's take a closer look at the normal and special element data structures and computation of the corresponding local $\mathbf{M}, \mathbf{D}$ and $\mathbf{K}$ matrices.

3.3.2   Normal Elements

Each normal element is a bicubic surface patch and hence is defined by 16 vertices (from the 8-connected neighborhood of the corresponding normal face) in the initial control mesh. Each normal element keeps a set of pointers to those vertices of the initial mesh which act as control points for the given element. For a normal element, the mass, damping and stiffness matrices are of size $(16, 16)$ and can be computed exactly by carrying out the necessary integrations analytically. The matrix $\mathbf{J}$ in Eqn.3.18, 3.20 and 3.22 needs to be replaced by $\mathbf{J}_p$ (of Eqn.3.2) for computation of the local $\mathbf{M}, \mathbf{D}$ and $\mathbf{K}$ matrices respectively of the corresponding normal element.

3.3.3   Special Elements

Each special element consists of an infinite number of bicubic patches in the limit. We have already described a recursive enumeration of the bicubic patches of a special element in Section 3.2.2. Let us now consider an arbitrary bicubic patch of the special element in some level j. The mass matrix $\mathbf{M}_s$ of this patch can be written as

$$\mathbf{M}_s = \mathbf{\Omega}_s^T \mathbf{M}_p \mathbf{\Omega}_s \qquad (3.28)$$

where $\mathbf{M}_p$ is the normal element mass matrix (scaled by a factor of $\frac{1}{4^j}$ to take into account of the area shrinkage in bicubic patches at higher level of subdivision) and

$\mathbf{\Omega}_s$ is the transformation matrix of the control points of that arbitrary patch from the corresponding control points in the initial mesh. The damping and stiffness matrices for the given bicubic patch can be derived in a similar fashion. These mass, damping and stiffness matrices from various levels of (local) subdivision can then be assembled to form the mass, damping and stiffness matrices of the special element. It may be noted that the stiffness energy due to plate terms diverges at the extraordinary points on the limit surface. We solve the problem using a slightly different approach than the one used in Halstead et al. [38]. When the area of the bicubic patch obtained via local subdivision of the initial mesh around an extraordinary vertex becomes smaller than the display resolution, the contribution from such a bicubic patch is ignored in computing the physical matrices of the corresponding special element. The number of extraordinary points in the limit surface is *very few*, and the above mentioned approximation is found to work well in practice.

3.3.4 Force Application

The force $\mathbf{f}(u, v, t)$ in Eqn.3.23 represents the net effect of all externally applied forces. The current implementation supports spring, inflation as well as image-based forces. However, other types of forces like repulsion forces, gravitational forces etc. can easily be implemented.

To apply spring forces, a spring of stiffness k can be connected from a point $\mathbf{d}_0$ to a point $\mathbf{x}_0$ on the limit surface (or, to the j-th level approximation mesh), the net applied spring force being

$$\mathbf{f}(\mathbf{x}, t) = \int_{\mathbf{x} \in S^j} k(\mathbf{d}_0 - \mathbf{s}(\mathbf{x}, t)) \delta(\mathbf{x} - \mathbf{x}_0) d\mathbf{x}, \tag{3.29}$$

where δ is the unit impulse function implying $\mathbf{f}(\mathbf{x}_0, t) = k|\mathbf{d}_0 - \mathbf{s}(\mathbf{x}_0, t)|$ and vanishes elsewhere on the surface. However, the δ function can be replaced with a smooth kernel to spread the force over a greater portion on the surface. The spring forces can be applied interactively using the computer mouse or the points from which forces need to be applied can be read in from a file.

To recover shapes from 3D image data, we synthesize image-based forces. A 3D edge detection is performed on a volume data set using the 3D Monga-Deriche(MD) operator [69] to produce a 3D potential field $P(x, y, z)$, which we use as an external potential for the model. The force distribution is then computed as

$$\mathbf{f}(x, y, z) = \lambda \frac{\nabla P(x, y, z)}{\| \nabla P(x, y, z) \|}, \tag{3.30}$$

where λ controls the strength of the force. The applied force on each vertex at the j-th approximation level is computed by trilinear interpolation for evaluating Eqn.3.23 in Cartesian coordinates. More sophisticated image-based forces which incorporate region-based information such as gradients of a thresholded fuzzy voxel classification can also be used to yield better and more accurate shape recovery. It may be noted that we can apply spring forces in addition with the image-based forces by placing points on the boundary of the region of interest in each slices of the 3D volume (MR, CT etc.) image data.

3.3.5 Discrete Dynamic Equation

The differential equation given by Eqn.2.5 is integrated through time by discretizing the time derivative of $\mathbf{p}$ over time steps Δt. The state of the dynamic subdivision surface at time $t + \Delta t$ is integrated using prior states at time t and $t - \Delta t$. An implicit time integration method is used in the current implementation where discrete derivatives of $\mathbf{p}$ are calculated using

$$\ddot{\mathbf{p}}(t + \Delta t) = \frac{\mathbf{p}(t + \Delta t) - 2\mathbf{p}(t) + \mathbf{p}(t - \Delta t)}{\Delta t^2}, \tag{3.31}$$

and

$$\dot{\mathbf{p}}(t + \Delta t) = \frac{\mathbf{p}(t + \Delta t) - \mathbf{p}(t - \Delta t)}{2\Delta t}. \tag{3.32}$$

The elemental mass, damping and stiffness matrices can be assembled to get the global mass, damping and stiffness matrix for the smooth subdivision surface model. However, we do not assemble these global sparse matrices explicitly for efficiency reasons. For the time varying stiffness matrix, we recompute $\mathbf{K}$ at each time step. Using Eqn.2.5, Eqn.3.31 and Eqn.3.32, the discrete equation of motion is obtained as

$$(2\mathbf{M} + \mathbf{D}\Delta t + 2\Delta t^2\mathbf{K})\mathbf{p}(t + \Delta t) = 2\Delta t^2\mathbf{f}_p(t + \Delta t) + (\mathbf{D}\Delta t - 2\mathbf{M})\mathbf{p}(t - \Delta t) + 4\mathbf{M}\mathbf{p}(t). \tag{3.33}$$

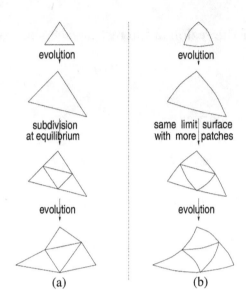

Figure 3.7. Model subdivision to increase the degrees of freedom : (a) evolution of the initial mesh, and (b) the corresponding limit surface evolution perceived by the user.

This linear system of equations is solved iteratively between each time step using the conjugate gradient method [34, 75].

3.3.6 Model Subdivision

The initialized model grows dynamically according to the equation of motion (Eqn.2.5). The degrees of freedom of the initialized model is equal to the number of control vertices in the initial mesh as mentioned earlier. When an equilibrium is achieved for the model, the number of control vertices can be increased by replacing the original initial mesh by a new initial mesh obtained through one step of Catmull-Clark subdivision. This increases the number of degrees of freedom to represent the same (deformed) smooth limit surface and a new equilibrium position for the model can be obtained. This process is depicted schematically in Fig.3.7. Model subdivision might be needed to obtain a very localized effect on a smooth limit surface. For a shape recovery application, one may start with a very simple initial model, and when an approximate shape is recovered, the degrees of freedom can be increased to obtain a new equilibrium position for the model with a better fit to the given data set. The error of fit criteria for the discrete data is based on distance between the data points and the points on the limit surface where the corresponding springs are attached. In the context of image-based forces, if the model energy does not change between successive iterations indicating an equilibrium for the given resolution, the degrees of freedom for the model can be increased by the above-mentioned replacement scheme until the model energy is sufficiently small and the change in model energy between successive iterations becomes less than a pre-specified tolerance.

3.4   Generalization of the Approach

The proposed approach can be generalized for other approximating subdivision schemes. However, a more general approach is presented in Chapter 5 for deriving the dynamic framework. Dynamic Catmull-Clark subdivision surface model is reformulated in Section 5.2 using this general approach. A dynamic framework for another popular approximating subdivision scheme namely, Loop's subdivision scheme, is also discussed in Chapter 5.

CHAPTER 4
DYNAMIC BUTTERFLY SUBDIVISION SURFACES

In the previous chapter, a dynamic framework has been presented for an approximating subdivision scheme namely, Catmull-Clark subdivision scheme. In this chapter, a dynamic framework is developed for (modified) butterfly subdivision scheme, which is an interpolatory subdivision technique. First, a brief overview of the (modified) butterfly subdivision scheme is presented. Next, a local parameterization technique for the limit surface obtained via (modified) butterfly subdivision is discussed. This parameterization scheme is then used to derive the dynamic model. The implementation details are also discussed.

4.1   Overview of the (Modified) Butterfly Subdivision Scheme

The butterfly subdivision scheme [30], like many other subdivision schemes used in geometric design literature/applications, starts with an initial triangular mesh which is also known as the control mesh. The vertices of the control mesh are known as the control points. In each step of subdivision, the initial (control) mesh is refined through the transformation of each triangular face into a patch with four *smaller* triangular faces. After one step of refinement, the new mesh in the *finer* level retains the vertices of each triangular face in the previous level and hence, interpolates the *coarser* mesh in the previous level. In addition, every edge in each triangular face

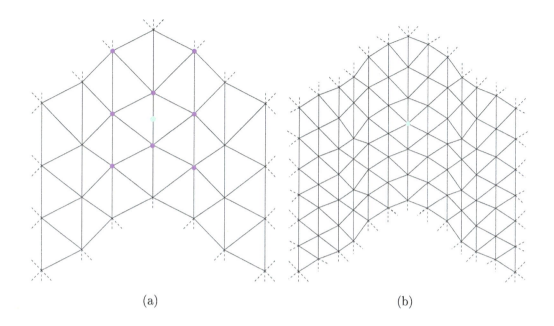

(a)   (b)

Figure 4.1. (a) The control polygon with triangular faces; (b) mesh obtained after one subdivision step using butterfly subdivision rules.

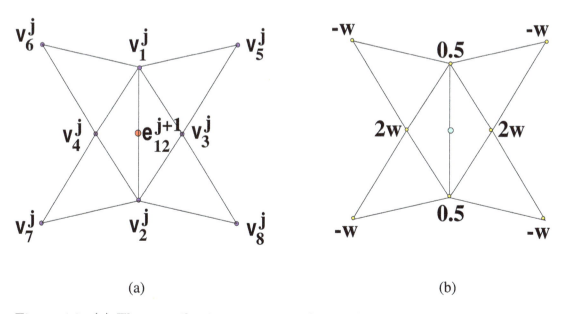

(a)   (b)

Figure 4.2. (a) The contributing vertices in the j-th level for the vertex in the j+1-th level corresponding to the edge between $\mathbf{v}_1^j$ and $\mathbf{v}_2^j$; (b) the weighing factors for different vertices.

is spilt by adding a new vertex whose position is obtained by an affine combination of the neighboring vertex positions in the coarser level. For instance, the mesh in Fig.4.1(b) is obtained by subdividing the initial mesh shown in Fig.4.1(a) once. It may be noted that all the newly introduced vertices corresponding to the edges in the original mesh have degree 6, whereas the position and degree of the original vertices do not change in the subdivided mesh.

In the original butterfly scheme, the new vertices corresponding to the edges in the previous level are obtained using an eight-point stencil as shown in Fig.4.2(a). To show how this stencil is used, a vertex to be introduced and the contributing vertices from the stencil are highlighted in Fig.4.1(a). The name of the scheme originated from the "butterfly"-like configuration of the contributing vertices. The weighing factors for different contributing vertex positions are shown in Fig.4.2(b). The vertex $\mathbf{e}_{12}^{j+1}$ in the $j+1$-th level of subdivision, corresponding to the edge connecting vertices $\mathbf{v}_1^j$ and $\mathbf{v}_2^j$ at level j, is obtained by

$$\mathbf{e}_{12}^{j+1} = 0.5(\mathbf{v}_1^j + \mathbf{v}_2^j) + 2w(\mathbf{v}_3^j + \mathbf{v}_4^j) - w(\mathbf{v}_5^j + \mathbf{v}_6^j + \mathbf{v}_7^j + \mathbf{v}_8^j), \qquad (4.1)$$

where $0 \leq w \leq 1$, and $\mathbf{v}_i^j$ denotes the position of the i-th vertex at the j-th level.

The butterfly subdivision scheme produces a smooth C^1 surface in the limit except at the *extraordinary* points corresponding to the *extraordinary* vertices (vertices with degree not equal to 6) in the initial mesh [109]. All the vertices introduced through subdivision have degree 6, and therefore, the number of extraordinary points in the smooth limit surface equals the number of extraordinary vertices in the initial

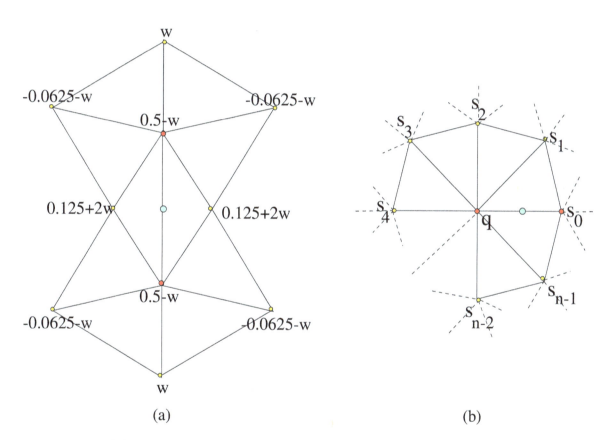

(a)   (b)

Figure 4.3. (a) The weighing factors of contributing vertex positions for an edge
connecting two vertices of degree 6; (b) the corresponding case when one vertex is of
degree n and the other is of degree 6.

mesh. Recently, this scheme has been modified by Zorin et al. [109] to obtain better smoothness properties at the extraordinary points. This modified scheme is known as *modified* butterfly subdivision technique. In Zorin et al. [109], all the edges have been categorized into three classes : (i) edges connecting two vertices of degree 6 (a 10 point stencil, as shown in Fig.4.3(a), is used to obtain the new vertex positions corresponding to these edges), (ii) edges connecting a vertex of degree 6 and a vertex of degree $n \neq 6$ (the corresponding stencil to obtain new vertex position is shown in Fig.4.3(b), where $q = .75$ is the weight associated with the vertex of degree $n \neq 6$, and $s_i = (0.25 + cos(2\pi i/n) + 0.5cos(4\pi i/n))/n$, $i = 0, 1, \ldots, n - 1$, are the weights associated with the vertices of degree 6), and (iii) edges connecting two vertices of degree $n \neq 6$. The last case can not occur except in the initial mesh as the newly introduced vertices are of degree 6, and the new vertex position in this last case is obtained by averaging the positions obtained through the use of stencil shown in Fig.4.3(b) at each of those two extraordinary vertices.

4.2   Formulation

In this section, a systematic formulation of the dynamic framework for the modified butterfly subdivision scheme is presented. Unlike the approximating schemes, the limit surface obtained via modified butterfly subdivision does not have any analytic expression even in a regular setting. Therefore, derivation of a local parameterization suitable for developing the dynamic framework for the limit surface is the key issue here which is discussed next.

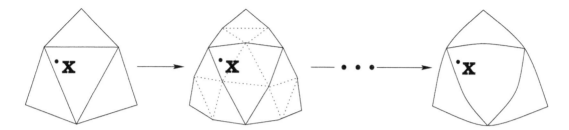

Figure 4.4. The smoothing effect of the subdivision process on the triangles of the initial mesh.

4.2.1 Local Parameterization

The smooth limit surface defined by the modified butterfly subdivision technique is of arbitrary topology where a global parameterization is impossible. Nevertheless, the limit surface can be locally parameterized over the domain defined by the initial mesh following a similar approach described in Lounsbery et al. [53]. The idea is to track any arbitrary point on the initial mesh across the meshes obtained via the subdivision process (see Fig.4.4 and Fig.4.5), so that a correspondence can be established between the point being tracked in the initial mesh and its image on the limit surface.

The modified butterfly subdivision scheme starts with an initial mesh consisting of a set of triangular faces. The recursive application of the subdivision rules smoothes out each triangular face, and in the limit, a smooth surface is obtained which can also be considered as a collection of smooth triangular patches. The subdivision process and the triangular decomposition of the limit surface is depicted in Fig.4.4. Note that, the limit surface can be represented by the same number of smooth triangular patches as that of the triangular faces in the initial mesh. Therefore, the limit surface

s can be expressed as

$$\mathbf{s} = \sum_{k=1}^{n} \mathbf{s}_k, \tag{4.2}$$

where n is the number of triangular faces in the initial mesh and $\mathbf{s}_k$ is the smooth triangular patch in the limit surface corresponding to the k-th triangular face in the initial mesh.

The stage is now set for describing the parameterization of the limit surface over the initial mesh. The process is best explained through the following example. A simple planar mesh shown in Fig.4.5(a) is chosen as the initial mesh. An arbitrary point **x** inside the triangular face abc is tracked over the meshes obtained through subdivision. The vertices in the initial mesh are darkly shaded in Fig.4.5. After one step of subdivision, the initial mesh is refined by addition of new vertices which are lightly shaded. Another subdivision step on this refined mesh leads to a finer mesh with introduction of new vertices which are unshaded. It may be noted that *any point inside the smooth triangular patch in the limit surface corresponding to the face abc in the initial mesh depends only on the vertices in the initial mesh which are within the 2-neighborhood of the vertices* **a**, **b** *and* **c** *due to the local nature of the subdivision process.* For example, the vertex **d**, introduced after first subdivision step, can be obtained using the 10 point stencil shown in Fig.4.3(a) on the edge ab. All the contributing vertices in the initial mesh are within the 1-neighborhood of the vertices **a** and **b**. A 10 point stencil can be used again in the next subdivision step on the edge db to obtain the vertex **g**. Some of the contributing vertices at this level of subdivision, for example, the (lightly shaded) 1-neighbors of the vertex **b** (except

64

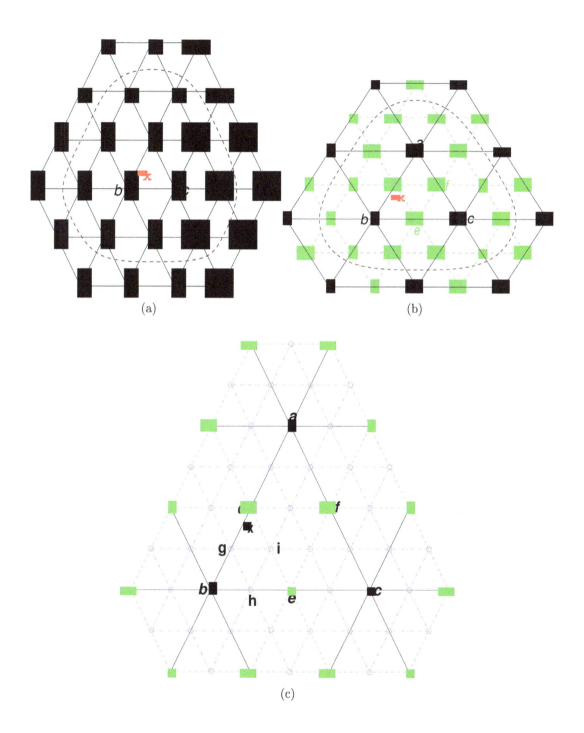

Figure 4.5. Tracking a point **x** through various levels of subdivision : (a) initial mesh, (b) the selected section (enclosed by dotted lines) of the mesh in (a), after one subdivision step, (c) the selected section of the mesh in (b), after another subdivision step.

d and **e**) in Fig.4.5(b), depend on some vertices in the initial mesh which are within the 2-neighborhood of the vertices **a**, **b** and **c** in the initial mesh.

In the rest of the formulation, superscripts are used to indicate the subdivision level. For example, $\mathbf{v}_{uvw}^j$ denotes the collection of vertices at level j which control the smooth patch in the limit surface corresponding to the triangular face uvw at the j-th level of subdivision. Let $\mathbf{v}_{abc}^0$ be the collection of vertices in the initial mesh which are within the 2-neighborhood of the vertices **a**, **b** and **c** (marked black in Fig.4.5(a)). Let the number of such vertices be r. Then, the vector $\mathbf{v}_{abc}^0$, which is the concatenation of the (x, y, z) positions for all the r vertices, is of dimension $3r$. These r vertices control the smooth triangular patch in the limit surface corresponding to the triangular face abc in the initial mesh. Now, there exists four subdivision matrices $(\mathbf{A}_{abc})_t$, $(\mathbf{A}_{abc})_l$, $(\mathbf{A}_{abc})_r$ and $(\mathbf{A}_{abc})_m$ of dimension $(3r, 3r)$ such that

$$
\begin{aligned}
\mathbf{v}_{adf}^1 &= (\mathbf{A}_{abc})_t \mathbf{v}_{abc}^0, \\
\mathbf{v}_{bed}^1 &= (\mathbf{A}_{abc})_l \mathbf{v}_{abc}^0, \\
\mathbf{v}_{cfe}^1 &= (\mathbf{A}_{abc})_r \mathbf{v}_{abc}^0, \\
\mathbf{v}_{def}^1 &= (\mathbf{A}_{abc})_m \mathbf{v}_{abc}^0,
\end{aligned}
\tag{4.3}
$$

where the subscripts t, l, r and m denote top, left, right and middle triangle positions respectively (indicating the relative position of the *new* triangle with respect to the *original* triangle), and $\mathbf{v}_{adf}^1, \mathbf{v}_{bed}^1, \mathbf{v}_{cfe}^1$ and $\mathbf{v}_{def}^1$ are the concatenation of the (x, y, z) positions for the vertices in the 2-neighborhood of the corresponding triangle in the newly obtained subdivided mesh. The new vertices in this level of subdivision are lightly shaded in Fig.4.5(b). The 2-neighborhood configuration of the vertices in the newly obtained triangles is exactly the same as that of the original triangle, hence local subdivision matrices are square and the vector dimensions on both sides of Eqn.4.3 are the same. This concept is further illustrated in Fig.4.6.

Carrying out one more level of subdivision, a new set of vertices which are unshaded in Fig.4.5(c) are obtained along with the old vertices. Adopting a similar approach as in the derivation of Eqn.4.3, it can be shown that

$$\mathbf{v}_{dgi}^2 = (\mathbf{A}_{bed})_t \mathbf{v}_{bed}^1$$

$$\mathbf{v}_{bhg}^2 = (\mathbf{A}_{bed})_l \mathbf{v}_{bed}^1$$

$$\mathbf{v}_{eih}^2 = (\mathbf{A}_{bed})_r \mathbf{v}_{bed}^1$$

$$\mathbf{v}_{ghi}^2 = (\mathbf{A}_{bed})_m \mathbf{v}_{bed}^1 \qquad (4.4)$$

The relative position of the triangular face dgi in Fig.4.5(c) with respect to the triangular face bed is topologically the same as of the triangular face adf in Fig.4.5(b) with respect to the triangular face abc. Therefore, one can write $(\mathbf{A}_{bed})_t = (\mathbf{A}_{abc})_t$. Using similar reasoning, Eqn.4.4 can be rewritten as

$$\mathbf{v}_{dgi}^2 = (\mathbf{A}_{bed})_t \mathbf{v}_{bed}^1 = (\mathbf{A}_{abc})_t \mathbf{v}_{bed}^1$$

$$\mathbf{v}_{bhg}^2 = (\mathbf{A}_{bed})_l \mathbf{v}_{bed}^1 = (\mathbf{A}_{abc})_l \mathbf{v}_{bed}^1$$

$$\mathbf{v}_{eih}^2 = (\mathbf{A}_{bed})_r \mathbf{v}_{bed}^1 = (\mathbf{A}_{abc})_r \mathbf{v}_{bed}^1$$

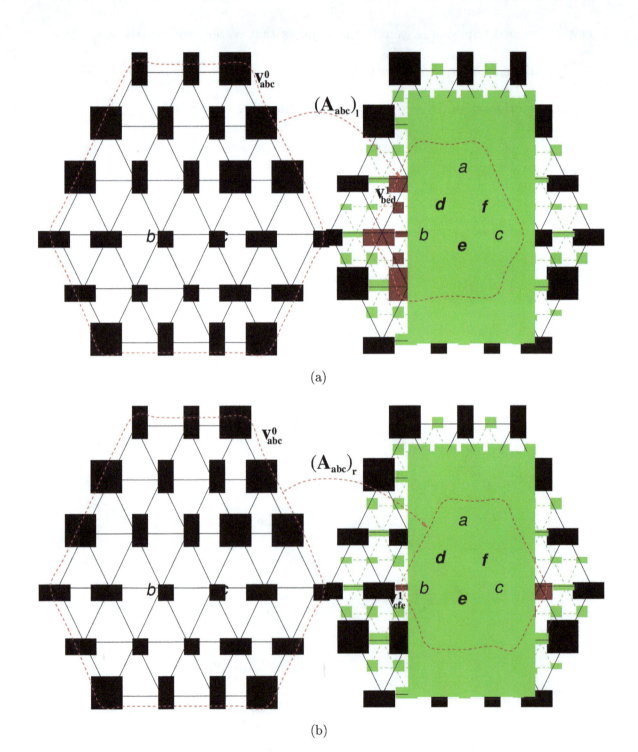

(a)

(b)

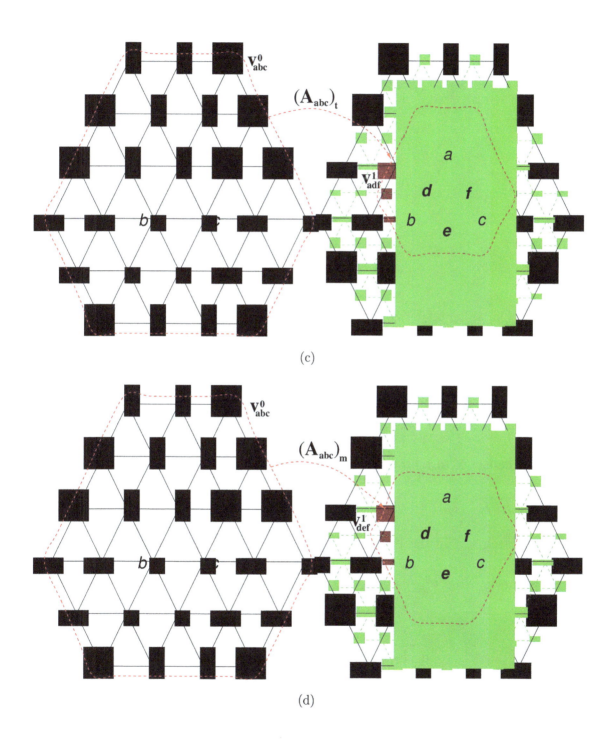

Figure 4.6. Different set of control points at a subdivided level obtained by applying different subdivision matrices on a given set of control points in a coarser mesh.

$$\mathbf{v}_{ghi}^2 = (\mathbf{A}_{bed})_m \mathbf{v}_{bed}^1 = (\mathbf{A}_{abc})_m \mathbf{v}_{bed}^1. \qquad (4.5)$$

Combining Eqn.4.3 and Eqn.4.5, it can be shown that

$$\mathbf{v}_{dgi}^2 = (\mathbf{A}_{abc})_t (\mathbf{A}_{abc})_l \mathbf{v}_{abc}^0,$$

$$\mathbf{v}_{bhg}^2 = (\mathbf{A}_{abc})_l (\mathbf{A}_{abc})_l \mathbf{v}_{abc}^0,$$

$$\mathbf{v}_{eih}^2 = (\mathbf{A}_{abc})_r (\mathbf{A}_{abc})_l \mathbf{v}_{abc}^0,$$

$$\mathbf{v}_{ghi}^2 = (\mathbf{A}_{abc})_m (\mathbf{A}_{abc})_l \mathbf{v}_{abc}^0. \qquad (4.6)$$

Let $\mathbf{x}$ be a point with barycentric coordinates $(\alpha_{abc}^0, \beta_{abc}^0, \gamma_{abc}^0)$ inside the triangular face abc. When the initial mesh is subdivided, $\mathbf{x}$ becomes a point inside the triangular face bed with barycentric coordinates $(\alpha_{bed}^1, \beta_{bed}^1, \gamma_{bed}^1)$. Another level of subdivision causes $\mathbf{x}$ to be included in the triangular face dgi with barycentric coordinates $(\alpha_{dgi}^2, \beta_{dgi}^2, \gamma_{dgi}^2)$. Let $\mathbf{s}_{abc}^j$ denote the j-th level approximation of the smooth triangular patch $\mathbf{s}_{abc}$ in the limit surface corresponding to the triangular face abc in the initial mesh. Now $\mathbf{v}_{abc}^0$ can be written as

$$\mathbf{v}_{abc}^0 = [\overbrace{a_x, b_x, c_x, \ldots}^{r}, \overbrace{a_y, b_y, c_y, \ldots}^{r}, \overbrace{a_z, b_z, c_z, \ldots}^{r}]^T$$

where the subscripts x, y and z indicate the x, y and z coordinates respectively of the corresponding vertex position. The expressions for $\mathbf{v}_{bed}^1$ and $\mathbf{v}_{dgi}^2$ can also be written in a similar manner. Next, the matrix $\mathbf{B}^0_{abc}$ can be constructed as follows:

$$\mathbf{B}^0_{abc}(\mathbf{x}) = \begin{bmatrix} \overbrace{\alpha^0_{abc}, \beta^0_{abc}, \gamma^0_{abc}, 0, \ldots, 0}^{r}, \overbrace{0, \ldots, 0}^{r}, \overbrace{0, \ldots, 0}^{r} \\ \overbrace{0, \ldots, 0}^{r}, \overbrace{\alpha^0_{abc}, \beta^0_{abc}, \gamma^0_{abc}, 0, \ldots, 0}^{r}, \overbrace{0, \ldots, 0}^{r} \\ \overbrace{0, \ldots, 0}^{r}, \overbrace{0, \ldots, 0}^{r}, \overbrace{\alpha^0_{abc}, \beta^0_{abc}, \gamma^0_{abc}, 0, \ldots, 0}^{r} \end{bmatrix}.$$

The matrices $\mathbf{B}^1_{bed}$ and $\mathbf{B}^2_{dgi}$ can also be constructed in a similar fashion. Now $\mathbf{s}^0_{abc}(\mathbf{x})$, $\mathbf{s}^1_{abc}(\mathbf{x})$, and $\mathbf{s}^2_{abc}(\mathbf{x})$ can be written as

$$\begin{aligned} \mathbf{s}^0_{abc}(\mathbf{x}) &= \mathbf{B}^0_{abc}(\mathbf{x})\mathbf{v}^0_{abc}, \\ \mathbf{s}^1_{abc}(\mathbf{x}) &= \mathbf{B}^1_{bed}(\mathbf{x})\mathbf{v}^1_{bed} = \mathbf{B}^1_{bed}(\mathbf{x})(\mathbf{A}_{abc})_l\mathbf{v}^0_{abc}, \\ \mathbf{s}^2_{abc}(\mathbf{x}) &= \mathbf{B}^2_{dgi}(\mathbf{x})\mathbf{v}^2_{dgi} = \mathbf{B}^2_{dgi}(\mathbf{x})(\mathbf{A}_{abc})_t\mathbf{v}^1_{bed} = \mathbf{B}^2_{dgi}(\mathbf{x})(\mathbf{A}_{abc})_t(\mathbf{A}_{abc})_l\mathbf{v}^0_{abc}. \end{aligned}$$
$$(4.7)$$

Proceeding in a similar way, the expression for $\mathbf{s}^j_{abc}(\mathbf{x})$, j-th level approximation of $\mathbf{s}_{abc}(\mathbf{x})$, is given by

$$\begin{aligned} \mathbf{s}^j_{abc}(\mathbf{x}) &= \mathbf{B}^j_{uvw}(\mathbf{x})\overbrace{(\mathbf{A}_{abc})_m \cdots (\mathbf{A}_{abc})_t(\mathbf{A}_{abc})_l}^{j}\mathbf{v}^0_{abc} \\ &= \mathbf{B}^j_{uvw}(\mathbf{x})(\mathbf{A}^j_{abc})\mathbf{v}^0_{abc} \\ &= \mathbf{B}^j_{abc}(\mathbf{x})\mathbf{v}^0_{abc}, \end{aligned}$$
$$(4.8)$$

where $\mathbf{x}$ is inside the triangular face uvw at level j (with an assumption that uvw is the triangular face in the *middle* with respect to its coarser level original triangular face in the previous level), $(\mathbf{A}_{abc}^{j}) = (\mathbf{A}_{abc})_m \cdots (\mathbf{A}_{abc})_t (\mathbf{A}_{abc})_l$ and $\mathbf{B}_{abc}^{j}(\mathbf{x}) = \mathbf{B}_{uvw}^{j}(\mathbf{x})(\mathbf{A}_{abc}^{j})$.

It may be noted that the sequence of applying $(\mathbf{A}_{abc})_t$, $(\mathbf{A}_{abc})_l$, $(\mathbf{A}_{abc})_r$ and $(\mathbf{A}_{abc})_m$

depends on the triangle inside which the tracked point $\mathbf{x}$ falls after each subdivision

step. Finally, the local parameterization process can be completed by writing

$$\mathbf{s}_{abc}(\mathbf{x}) = (\lim_{j \to \infty} \mathbf{B}_{abc}^{j}(\mathbf{x}))\mathbf{v}_{abc}^{0} = \mathbf{B}_{abc}(\mathbf{x})\mathbf{v}_{abc}^{0}. \tag{4.9}$$

In the above equation, $\mathbf{B}_{abc}$ is the collection of basis functions at the vertices of

$\mathbf{v}_{abc}^{0}$. It may also be noted that the modified butterfly subdivision scheme is a sta-

tionary subdivision process, and hence new vertex positions are obtained by affine

combinations of nearby vertices. This guarantees that each row of the matrices

$(\mathbf{A}_{abc})_t$, $(\mathbf{A}_{abc})_l$, $(\mathbf{A}_{abc})_r$ and $(\mathbf{A}_{abc})_m$ sums to one. The largest eigenvalue of such ma-

trices is 1 and therefore the limit in Eqn.4.9 exists. Now, assuming the triangular

face abc is the k-th face in the initial mesh, Eqn.4.9 can be rewritten as

$$\mathbf{s}_k(\mathbf{x}) = \mathbf{B}_k(\mathbf{x})\mathbf{v}_k^{0} = \mathbf{B}_k(\mathbf{x})\mathbf{A}_k\mathbf{p}, \tag{4.10}$$

where $\mathbf{p}$ is the concatenation of the (x,y,z) positions of all the vertices in the initial

mesh and the matrix $\mathbf{A}_k$, when post-multiplied by $\mathbf{p}$, selects the vertices $\mathbf{v}_k^{0}$ controlling

the k-th smooth triangular patch in the limit surface. If there are t vertices in the

initial mesh and r of them control the k-th patch, then $\mathbf{p}$ is a vector of dimension $3t$,

$\mathbf{A}_k$ is a matrix of dimension $(3r, 3t)$, and $\mathbf{B}_k(\mathbf{x})$ is a matrix of dimension $(3, 3r)$.

Combining Eqn.4.2 and Eqn.4.10, it can be shown that

$$\mathbf{s}(\mathbf{x}) = (\sum_{k=1}^{n} \mathbf{B}_k(\mathbf{x})\mathbf{A}_k)\mathbf{p} = \mathbf{J}(\mathbf{x})\mathbf{p}, \qquad (4.11)$$

where $\mathbf{J}$, a matrix of dimension $(3, 3t)$, is the collection of basis functions for the corresponding vertices in the initial mesh. The vector $\mathbf{p}$ is also known as the degrees of freedom vector of the smooth limit surface $\mathbf{s}$.

4.2.2 Dynamics

An expression of the limit surface obtained via modified butterfly subdivision process is derived in the last section. Now a dynamic framework for the limit surface can be derived using this expression. The derivation of the dynamic model from this point is exactly similar in spirit as that of the dynamic Catmull-Clark subdivision model presented in Section 3.2.4. The vertex positions in the initial mesh defining the smooth limit surface $\mathbf{s}$ are treated as a function of time in order to embed the modified butterfly subdivision model in a dynamic framework. The velocity of this surface model can be expressed as

$$\dot{\mathbf{s}}(\mathbf{x}, \mathbf{p}) = \mathbf{J}(\mathbf{x})\dot{\mathbf{p}}, \qquad (4.12)$$

where an overstruck dot denotes a time derivative and $\mathbf{x} \in S^0$, S^0 being the domain defined by the initial mesh. As in the case of the dynamic Catmull-Clark subdivision surfaces, the Lagrangian equation of motion (Eqn.2.1) is used to derive the dynamic modified butterfly subdivision surface model.

Let μ be the mass density function of the surface. Then the kinetic energy of the surface is

$$T \;=\; \frac{1}{2}\int_{\mathbf{x}\in S^0}\mu(\mathbf{x})\dot{\mathbf{s}}^T(\mathbf{x})\dot{\mathbf{s}}(\mathbf{x})d\mathbf{x} \;=\; \frac{1}{2}\dot{\mathbf{p}}^T\mathbf{M}\dot{\mathbf{p}}, \qquad (4.13)$$

where (using Eqn.4.12) $\mathbf{M}=\int_{\mathbf{x}\in S^0}\mu(\mathbf{x})\mathbf{J}^T(\mathbf{x})\mathbf{J}(\mathbf{x})d\mathbf{x}$ is the mass matrix of dimension $(3t,3t)$. Similarly, let γ be the damping density function of the surface. The dissipation energy is

$$F \;=\; \frac{1}{2}\int_{\mathbf{x}\in S^0}\gamma(\mathbf{x})\dot{\mathbf{s}}^T(\mathbf{x})\dot{\mathbf{s}}(\mathbf{x})d\mathbf{x} \;=\; \frac{1}{2}\dot{\mathbf{p}}^T\mathbf{D}\dot{\mathbf{p}}, \qquad (4.14)$$

where $\mathbf{D}=\int_{\mathbf{x}\in S^0}\gamma(\mathbf{x})\mathbf{J}^T(\mathbf{x})\mathbf{J}(\mathbf{x})d\mathbf{x}$ is the damping matrix of dimension $(3t,3t)$. The potential energy of the smooth limit surface can be expressed as

$$U \;=\; \frac{1}{2}\mathbf{p}^T\mathbf{K}\mathbf{p}, \qquad (4.15)$$

where $\mathbf{K}$ is the stiffness matrix of dimension $(3t,3t)$ obtained by assigning various internal energies to a discretized approximation of the limit surface and is detailed in Section 4.3.

Using the expressions for the kinetic, dissipation and potential energy in Eqn.2.1, the same motion equation as in Eqn.2.5 can be obtained. The generalized force vector

$\mathbf{f}_p$ can be obtained is a similar fashion described in Section 3.2.4 and is given by

$$\mathbf{f}_p = \int_{\mathbf{x} \in S^0} \mathbf{J}^T(\mathbf{x})\mathbf{f}(\mathbf{x}, t)d\mathbf{x}. \tag{4.16}$$

4.2.3 Multilevel Dynamics

The initial mesh of the dynamic modified butterfly subdivision surface model can be subdivided to increase the degrees of freedom for model representation. The situation is exactly similar to that of the dynamic Catmull-Clark subdivision surface model as described in Section 3.2.5 and a similar example is used for illustration. After one step of modified butterfly subdivision, the initial degrees of freedom $\mathbf{p}$ (refer to Eqn.4.11 and Eqn.4.12) in the dynamic system is replaced by a larger number of degrees of freedom $\mathbf{q}$, where $\mathbf{q} = \mathbf{Bp}$. $\mathbf{B}$ is a global subdivision matrix of size $(3s, 3t)$ whose entries are uniquely determined by the weights used in the modified butterfly subdivision scheme (see Section 4.1 for the weights). Thus, $\mathbf{p}$, expressed as a function of $\mathbf{q}$, can be written as

$$\mathbf{p} = (\mathbf{B}^T\mathbf{B})^{-1}\mathbf{B}^T\mathbf{q} = \mathbf{B}^\dagger\mathbf{q}, \tag{4.17}$$

where $\mathbf{B}^\dagger = (\mathbf{B}^T\mathbf{B})^{-1}\mathbf{B}^T$. Therefore, Eqn.4.11 and Eqn.4.12 is modified as

$$\mathbf{s}(\mathbf{x}) = (\mathbf{J}(\mathbf{x})\mathbf{B}^\dagger)\mathbf{q}, \tag{4.18}$$

and

$$\dot{\mathbf{s}}(\mathbf{x}, \mathbf{q}) = (\mathbf{J}(\mathbf{x})\mathbf{B}^\dagger)\dot{\mathbf{q}}, \tag{4.19}$$

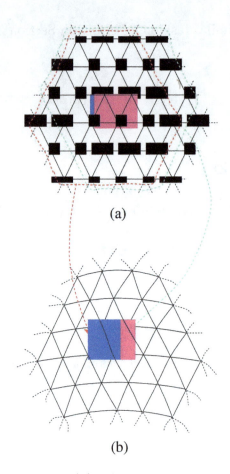

(a)

(b)

Figure 4.7. (a) An initial mesh, and (b) the corresponding limit surface. The domains of the shaded elements in the limit surface are the corresponding triangular faces in the initial mesh. The encircled vertices in (a) are the degrees of freedom for the corresponding element.

respectively. The motion equation, explicitly expressed as a function of $\mathbf{q}$, can be written as

$$\mathbf{M}_q\ddot{\mathbf{q}} + \mathbf{D}_q\dot{\mathbf{q}} + \mathbf{K}_q\mathbf{q} = \mathbf{f}_q, \tag{4.20}$$

where $\mathbf{M}_q = \int_{\mathbf{x} \in S^1} \mu(\mathbf{x})(\mathbf{B}^\dagger)^T \mathbf{J}^T(\mathbf{x})\mathbf{J}(\mathbf{x})\mathbf{B}^\dagger d\mathbf{x}$, S^1 being the domain defined by the newly obtained subdivided mesh. The derivations of $\mathbf{D}_q$, $\mathbf{K}_q$ and $\mathbf{f}_q$ are similar.

4.3   Finite Element Implementation

In the previous section, the smooth limit surface obtained via modified butterfly subdivision process is expressed as a function of the control vertex positions in its initial mesh; mass and damping distribution, internal deformation energy and forces are assigned to the limit surface in order to develop the corresponding physical model. In this section, the implementation of this physical model is detailed. It may be noted that even though the formulation of the dynamic framework for modified butterfly subdivision scheme is similar to that of Catmull-Clark subdivision scheme once the local parameterization is derived, the finite element implementation is totally different as the limit surface does not have any analytic expression in case of the modified butterfly subdivision scheme.

In Section 4.2 it was pointed out that the smooth limit surface obtained by the recursive application of the modified butterfly subdivision rules can be represented by a set of smooth triangular patches, each of which is represented by a finite element. The shape (basis) function of this finite element is obtained by smoothing a hat function through repeated application of the modified butterfly subdivision rules. The number of finite elements in the smooth limit surface is equal to the number of triangular faces in the initial mesh as mentioned earlier (refer Fig.4.4 and 4.7). A detailed discussion on how to derive the mass, damping and stiffness matrices for these elements is presented next. These elemental matrices can be assembled to obtain the global physical matrices $\mathbf{M}$, $\mathbf{D}$ and $\mathbf{K}$, and a numerical solution to the governing second-order differential equation as given by Eqn.2.5 can be obtained using finite element analysis techniques [42]. The same example as in Section 4.2 (refer Fig.4.5) is used to develop the related concepts. The concept of elements along with the control vertices and their corresponding domains is further illustrated in Fig.4.7.

Now it will be shown how to derive the mass, damping and stiffness matrices for the element corresponding to the triangular face abc in Fig.4.5. The derivations hold for any element in general.

4.3.1   Elemental Mass and Damping matrices

The mass matrix for the element given by s_{abc} (Eqn.4.9) can be written as

$$\mathbf{M}_{abc} = \int_{\mathbf{x} \in s_{abc}} \mu(\mathbf{x}) \{\mathbf{B}_{abc}(\mathbf{x})\}^T \{\mathbf{B}_{abc}(\mathbf{x})\} d\mathbf{x}. \qquad (4.21)$$

However, from Eqn.4.9 it is known that the basis functions corresponding to the vertices in $\mathbf{v}_{abc}^0$ which are stored as entries in $\mathbf{B}_{abc}$ are obtained as a limiting process. These basis functions do not have any analytic form, hence computing the inner product of such basis functions as needed in Eqn.4.21 is a challenging problem. In Lounsbery et al. [53], an outline is provided on the computation of these inner products without performing any integration. In this dissertation, a different yet simpler approach is developed to solve this problem. The smooth triangular patch in the limit surface corresponding to the face abc in the initial mesh is approximated by a triangular mesh with 4^j faces obtained after j levels of subdivision of the original triangular face abc (each subdivision step splits one triangular face into 4 triangular faces). Then the mass matrix can be expressed as

$$\mathbf{M}_{abc} = \sum_{i=1}^{4^j} \int_{\mathbf{x}\in\Delta_i} \mu(\mathbf{x})\{\mathbf{B}^j_{abc}(\mathbf{x})\}^T\{\mathbf{B}^j_{abc}(\mathbf{x})\}d\mathbf{x}. \qquad (4.22)$$

The j-th level approximation of the corresponding basis functions can be explicitly evaluated (refer Eqn.4.8 for an expression of $\mathbf{B}^j_{abc}$). An important point to note is that Eqn.4.8 involves several matrix multiplications and hence can be very expensive to evaluate. However, the matrix $(\mathbf{A}^j_{abc})(= (\mathbf{A}_{abc})_m \cdots (\mathbf{A}_{abc})_t(\mathbf{A}_{abc})_l)$ in Eqn.4.8 encodes how vertices in the 2-neighborhood of the triangular face uvw at level j are related to the vertices in the 2-neighborhood of the triangular face abc in the initial mesh. In the implementation, how a new vertex is obtained from the contributing vertices in its immediate predecessor level is tracked. The information stored in $(\mathbf{A}^j_{abc})$ can be obtained by tracking the contributions from level j to level 0 recursively. Thus the entries of $(\mathbf{A}^j_{abc})$ can be determined without forming any local subdivision matrices and thereby avoiding subsequent matrix multiplications.

By choosing a sufficiently high value of j, a reasonably good approximation of the elemental mass matrices is achieved. The computations involved in evaluating the integrals in Eqn.4.22 are eliminated by using discrete mass density function which has non-zero values only at the vertex positions of the j-th subdivision level mesh. Therefore, the approximation of the mass matrix for the element can be written as

$$\mathbf{M}_{abc} = \sum_{i=1}^{k} \mu(\mathbf{v}^j_i)\{\mathbf{B}^j_{abc}(\mathbf{v}^j_i)\}^T\{\mathbf{B}^j_{abc}(\mathbf{v}^j_i)\}, \qquad (4.23)$$

where k is the number of vertices in the triangular mesh with 4^j faces. This approximation has been found to be very effective and efficient for implementation purposes. The elemental damping matrix can be obtained in a similar fashion.

4.3.2   Elemental Stiffness Matrix

The internal energy is assigned to each element in the limit surface, thereby defining the internal energy of the smooth subdivision surface model. A similar approach as in the derivation of the elemental mass and damping matrix is taken and the internal energy is assigned to a j-th level approximation of the element.

Three types of internal energy are used – tension, stiffness and spring energy. For the examples used throughout the paper, this energy at the j-th level of approximation can be written as

$$E_{abc} \approx E_{abc}^j = (E_{abc}^j)_t + (E_{abc}^j)_{st} + (E_{abc}^j)_{sp}, \tag{4.24}$$

where the subscripts t, st and sp denote tension, stiffness and spring respectively.

The expression for the tension energy, which is essentially equivalent to the first order strain (membrane) energy [96], is

$$\begin{aligned}
(E_{abc}^j)_t &= \frac{1}{2} k_t \sum_\Omega |\mathbf{v}_l^j - \mathbf{v}_m^j|^2 \\
&= \frac{1}{2} k_t \{\mathbf{v}_{abc}^j\}^T (\mathbf{K}_{abc}^j)_t \{\mathbf{v}_{abc}^j\},
\end{aligned} \tag{4.25}$$

where k_t is a constant, $\mathbf{v}_l^j$ and $\mathbf{v}_m^j$, the l-th and m-th vertex in the j-th level mesh, are in the 1-neighborhood of each other, Ω is the domain defined by all such vertex pairs, and $\mathbf{v}_{abc}^{j}$ is the concatenation of the (x,y,z) positions of all the vertices in the j-th subdivision level of the triangular face abc in the initial mesh.

Similarly, the expression for stiffness energy, which is equivalent to the second order strain (thin plate) energy [96], can be written as

$$
\begin{aligned}
(E_{abc}^{j})_{st} &= \frac{1}{2}k_{st}\sum_{\Omega}|\mathbf{v}_{l}^{j} - 2\mathbf{v}_{m}^{j} + \mathbf{v}_{n}^{j}|^{2} \\
&= \frac{1}{2}k_{st}\{\mathbf{v}_{abc}^{j}\}^{T}(\mathbf{K}_{abc}^{j})_{st}\{\mathbf{v}_{abc}^{j}\},
\end{aligned} \tag{4.26}
$$

where $\mathbf{v}_{l}^{j}$, $\mathbf{v}_{m}^{j}$ and $\mathbf{v}_{n}^{j}$ are the three vertices of a triangular face. The summation involves three terms corresponding to each triangular face, and is over all the triangular faces in the mesh at the j-th level of subdivision.

Finally, a spring energy term is added which is given by

$$
\begin{aligned}
(E_{abc}^{j})_{sp} &= \frac{1}{2}\sum_{\Omega}\frac{(k_{lm})_{sp}(|\mathbf{v}_{l}^{j} - \mathbf{v}_{m}^{j}| - \ell_{lm})}{|\mathbf{v}_{l}^{j} - \mathbf{v}_{m}^{j}|}(\mathbf{v}_{l}^{j} - \mathbf{v}_{m}^{j}) \\
&= \frac{1}{2}\{\mathbf{v}_{abc}^{j}\}^{T}(\mathbf{K}_{abc}^{j})_{sp}\{\mathbf{v}_{abc}^{j}\},
\end{aligned} \tag{4.27}
$$

where $(k_{lm})_{sp}$ is the spring constant, Ω is the domain as in Eqn.4.25 and ℓ_{lm} is the natural length of the spring connected between $\mathbf{v}_{l}^{j}$ and $\mathbf{v}_{m}^{j}$. It may be noted that the entries in $(\mathbf{K}_{abc}^{j})_{sp}$ depend on the distance between the connected vertices and hence, $(\mathbf{K}_{abc}^{j})_{sp}$, unlike other elemental matrices, is a function of time which needs to be recomputed in each time step.

Combining the expressions for tension, stiffness and spring energy, it can be shown that

$$
\begin{aligned}
E_{abc}^{j} &= \frac{1}{2}\{\mathbf{v}_{abc}^{j}\}^{T}\{k_{t}(\mathbf{K}_{abc}^{j})_{t} + k_{st}(\mathbf{K}_{abc}^{j})_{st} + (\mathbf{K}_{abc}^{j})_{sp}\}\{\mathbf{v}_{abc}^{j}\} \\
&= \frac{1}{2}\{\mathbf{v}_{abc}^{j}\}^{T}(\mathbf{K}_{abc}^{j})\{\mathbf{v}_{abc}^{j}\} \\
&= \frac{1}{2}\{(\mathbf{A}_{abc}^{j})\{\mathbf{v}_{abc}^{0}\}\}^{T}(\mathbf{K}_{abc}^{j})(\mathbf{A}_{abc}^{j})\{\mathbf{v}_{abc}^{0}\} \\
&= \frac{1}{2}\{\mathbf{v}_{abc}^{0}\}^{T}\{(\mathbf{A}_{abc}^{j})^{T}(\mathbf{K}_{abc}^{j})(\mathbf{A}_{abc}^{j})\}\{\mathbf{v}_{abc}^{0}\},
\end{aligned}
\tag{4.28}
$$

where $(\mathbf{A}_{abc}^{j})$ and $\mathbf{v}_{abc}^{0}$ are same as in Eqn.4.8. Therefore, the expression for the elemental stiffness matrix is given by

$$
\mathbf{K}_{abc} = (\mathbf{A}_{abc}^{j})^{T}(\mathbf{K}_{abc}^{j})(\mathbf{A}_{abc}^{j}).
\tag{4.29}
$$

It may be noted that the matrix multiplications for constructing $\mathbf{K}_{abc}$ are avoided in the implementation by following the same technique described in Section 4.3.1.

4.3.3 Other Implementation Issues

The techniques of applying synthesized forces on the smooth limit surface obtained via modified butterfly subdivision process are similar to those described in Section 3.3.4 in the context of dynamic Catmull-Clark subdivision surface model. The techniques of model subdivision and discrete dynamic equation derivation are also the same.

4.4   Generalization of the Approach

The proposed approach of deriving the dynamic framework for modified butter-fly subdivision scheme is generalized for other interpolatory subdivision schemes in the next chapter, Chapter 5.

CHAPTER 5
UNIFIED DYNAMIC FRAMEWORK FOR SUBDIVISION SURFACES

Dynamic framework for specific subdivision schemes was presented in the last two chapters. In Chapter 3, Catmull-Clark subdivision scheme, a representative of the approximating subdivision schemes, is embedded in a physics-based modeling environment. In Chapter 4, a dynamic framework is provided for the modified butterfly subdivision scheme, a popular interpolatory subdivision technique. In this chapter, a unified approach is presented for embedding any subdivision scheme in a dynamic framework.

5.1   Overview of the Unified Approach

The key concept of the unified approach is the ability to express the smooth limit surface generated by a subdivision scheme as a collection of a single type of finite elements. The type of this finite element depends on the subdivision scheme involved. For example, the limit surface generated by the Catmull-Clark subdivision scheme can be expressed as a collection a quadrilateral finite element patches. This approach differs form the one taken in Chapter 3 where the limit surface was a collection of normal elements (corresponding to the quadrilateral bicubic B-spline patches away from the extraordinary points) and special elements (corresponding to the n-sided patches near extraordinary vertices of degree n). This concept will be further elaborated in the next few sections.

The unified approach adopts two different strategies depending on the subdivision scheme involved. One strategy is for the approximating schemes, whose limit surface is some type of B-spline surface away from the extraordinary points, and the other is for the interpolatory subdivision schemes, where the limit surface does not have any analytical expression. It may be recalled that recursive subdivision is a method for smoothing polyhedra, and hence corresponding to each n-sided face in the control mesh, there would be a smooth n-sided patch in the limit surface in general. For example, the control mesh (after at most one subdivision step) of the Catmull-Clark subdivision scheme consists of quadrilateral faces, which when smoothed through subdivision lead to quadrilateral patches in the limit surface (see Fig.5.1(b)). In the case of approximating subdivision schemes, the faces which do not contain any extraordinary vertex lead to spline patches with analytic expressions. On the other hand, faces which have one extraordinary vertex, lead to patches whose analytic expressions are difficult to determine. Continuing the example with the Catmull-Clark subdivision scheme, the faces without extraordinary vertices lead to quadrilateral bicubic B-spline patches in the limit, whereas the faces with one extraordinary vertex lead to quadrilateral patches whose analytic expressions are difficult to obtain. In Chapter 3, n such adjacent patches corresponding to an extraordinary vertex of degree n are effectively combined together to obtain an expression for the resulting n-sided patch (see Fig.5.1(a)). Recently, Stam [90, 91] has introduced schemes for exactly evaluating the limit surface, even near the extraordinary points, for approximating subdivision schemes. Analytic expressions for the patches resulting from smoothing faces with an extraordinary vertex can be obtained using these schemes. Therefore, the limit surface can be expressed as a collection of a single patch type, and consequently a single type of finite element can be used to provide the dynamic framework for the approximating subdivision schemes. This unified framework for approximating subdivision schemes is fully worked out in this chapter for Catmull-Clark and Loop subdivision schemes and a general outline is also presented on how to carry out the same strategy for other approximating subdivision schemes.

The limit surface resulting from an interpolatory subdivision scheme does not have an analytic expression in general, and hence a strategy similar to the one adopted in Chapter 4 needs to be used. An outline of the strategy to be used for interpolatory subdivision schemes is also presented in this chapter.

5.2   Unified Dynamic Framework for Catmull-Clark Subdivision Surfaces

A systematic formulation along with the implementation details of the unified dynamic framework for Catmull-Clark subdivision surfaces is presented in this section. The key difference between the framework developed in Chapter 3 and the one presented here is the representation of the limit surface, which leads to different types of finite elements used for developing the dynamic framework. This is illustrated with a schematic diagram in Fig.5.1.

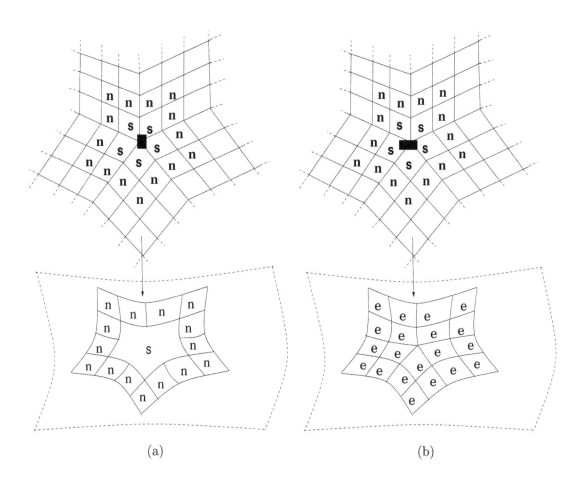

(a)   (b)

Figure 5.1. A control mesh with an extraordinary vertex of degree 5 and the corresponding limit surface : (a) using the concepts developed in Chapter 3, where the limit surface consists of quadrilateral normal elements and a pentagonal special element; (b) using the unified concept developed in this chapter, where the limit surface consists of one single type of quadrilateral finite element.

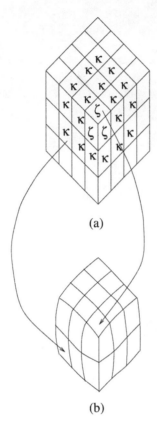

(a)

(b)

Figure 5.2. In Catmull-Clark subdivision, each non-boundary quadrilateral face in the control mesh has a corresponding quadrilateral patch in the limit surface : (a) control mesh, (b) limit surface.

Following the concepts developed in Chapter 3, the limit surface of the control mesh shown in Fig.5.1, consists of quadrilateral bicubic B-spline patches corresponding to the faces marked 'n' (faces with no extraordinary points), and a pentagonal patch corresponding to the faces marked 's' (faces having one extraordinary vertex of degree 5) (Fig.5.1(a)). However, in this section, it will be shown that the entire limit surface can be expressed as a collection of quadrilateral patches as illustrated in Fig.5.1(b) using the schemes proposed by Stam [90]. Next, the local parameterization of the limit surface is described in order to develop the unified dynamic framework.

5.2.1   Local Parameterization

As mentioned earlier, the control mesh (after at most one subdivision step) for the Catmull-Clark subdivision scheme consists of quadrilateral faces which lead to quadrilateral patches in the limit surface. For the sake of simplicity, it is assumed that each face has at most one extraordinary vertex. If this assumption is violated, then one more subdivision step needs to be performed on the current control mesh in order to obtain a new control mesh on which the following analysis can be carried out. The number of quadrilateral patches in the limit surface is equal to the number of non-boundary quadrilateral faces in the control mesh (Fig.5.2). Therefore, the smooth limit surface **s** can be expressed as

$$\mathbf{s} = \sum_{l=1}^{n} \mathbf{s}_l, \tag{5.1}$$

where n is the number of non-boundary faces in the control mesh and $\mathbf{s}_l$ is the smooth quadrilateral patch corresponding to the l-th non-boundary quadrilateral face in the control mesh. Each of these quadrilateral patches can be parameterized over the corresponding non-boundary quadrilateral face in the control mesh. However, since a quadrilateral face can easily be parameterized over a $[0,1]^2$ domain, each quadrilateral patch is locally parameterized over the domain $[0,1]^2$.

The non-boundary quadrilateral faces are of two types : (a) faces having no extraordinary vertices (dubbed as "regular" faces in Section 3.2.1, marked as κ in Fig.5.2(a)) and (b) faces with one extraordinary vertex (dubbed as "irregular" faces in Section 3.2.2, marked as ζ in Fig.5.2(a)). If there are m regular and $n-m$ irregular faces, then Eqn.5.1 can be rewritten as

$$\mathbf{s} = \sum_{i=1}^{m} \mathbf{s}_i + \sum_{j=1}^{n-m} \mathbf{s}_j, \tag{5.2}$$

where $\mathbf{s}_i$ is the quadrilateral patch corresponding to the i-th regular face and $\mathbf{s}_j$ is the quadrilateral patch corresponding to the j-th irregular face.

The quadrilateral patch in the limit surface corresponding to each regular face is a bicubic B-spline patch, which is defined over $[0,1]^2$. The set of control vertices defining this bicubic B-spline patch can be obtained using the adjacent face information (refer to Section 3.2.1 and Fig.3.1 in Chapter 3). Therefore, the quadrilateral patches in the smooth limit surface corresponding to the regular faces in the control mesh can be easily expressed analytically, which are essentially bicubic B-spline patches defined by 16 control vertices over a $[0,1]^2$ domain. The analytic expression for the quadrilateral patch corresponding to the regular face i is given by

$$
\begin{aligned}
\mathbf{s}_i &= \mathbf{J}_b(u,v)\mathbf{p}_i \\
&= (\mathbf{J}_b(u,v)\mathbf{A}_i)\mathbf{p} \\
&= \mathbf{J}_i(u,v)\mathbf{p},
\end{aligned}
\tag{5.3}
$$

where $0 \le u, v \le 1$, $\mathbf{J}_b(u,v)$ is the collection of the bicubic B-spline basis functions, $\mathbf{p}_i$ is the concatenation of the 16 control vertex positions defining the bicubic B-spline patch, $\mathbf{A}_i$ is a selection matrix which when multiplied with $\mathbf{p}$, the concatenation of all the control vertex positions defining the smooth limit surface, selects the corresponding set of control vertices, and $\mathbf{J}_i(u,v) = \mathbf{J}_b(u,v)\mathbf{A}_i$.

The analytic expression of the quadrilateral patches corresponding to the irregular faces in the control mesh was difficult to derive, and hence an alternative approach was taken in Mandal et al. [57, 60] and Qin et al. [76] as well as in Chapter 3. However, very recently an efficient scheme for evaluating Catmull-Clark subdivision surfaces at arbitrary parameter values was proposed by Stam [90]. The proposed approach, involving eigen-analysis of the subdivision matrix, leads to an analytic expression of a quadrilateral patch parameterized over an irregular face. Following the scheme developed by Stam [90], the quadrilateral patch corresponding to the irregular face j is given by

$$
\begin{aligned}
\mathbf{s}_j &= \mathbf{J}_{d_k}(u,v)\mathbf{p}_j \\
&= (\mathbf{J}_{d_k}(u,v)\mathbf{A}_j)\mathbf{p} \\
&= \mathbf{J}_j(u,v)\mathbf{p},
\end{aligned}
\tag{5.4}
$$

where $0 \leq u,v \leq 1$ as before. $\mathbf{J}_{d_k}(u,v)$ is the collection of basis functions for the corresponding quadrilateral patch in the smooth limit surface. The subscript d_k is used to denote the fact that the irregular face has an extraordinary vertex of degree k. The detailed derivation and the analytic expressions of these basis functions involving the eigenvalues and eigenvectors of the subdivision matrix can be found in Stam [90]. The rest of the notations used in Eqn.5.4 have the usual meaning : $\mathbf{p}_j$ is the concatenation of the $2k+8$ control vertices defining the quadrilateral patch in the

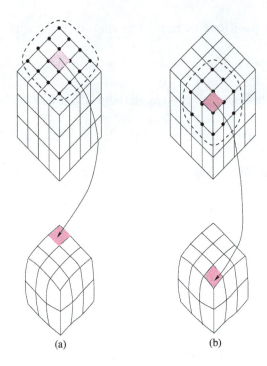

Figure 5.3. (a) The marked 16 control vertices define the shaded quadrilateral patch associated with the shaded regular face in the control mesh; (b) the marked 14 control vertices define the shaded quadrilateral patch associated with the shaded irregular face in the control mesh.

limit surface, $\mathbf{p}$ is the concatenation of all the control vertex positions defining the smooth limit surface, $\mathbf{A}_j$ is a selection matrix which when multiplied with $\mathbf{p}$ selects the corresponding set of control vertices, and $\mathbf{J}_j(u,v) = \mathbf{J}_{d_k}(u,v)\mathbf{A}_j$.

It may be noted that the number of control vertices in the initial mesh defining a quadrilateral patch in the smooth limit surface is $2k + 8$, where $k = 4$ in case the associated quadrilateral face in the control mesh is regular, or $k =$ degree of the extraordinary vertex if the associated quadrilateral face is irregular. For example, the shaded quadrilateral patch is associated with the shaded regular face in Fig.5.3(a), and the 16 control vertices defining this patch (which is actually a bicubic B-spline patch) are marked. Similarly, the shaded quadrilateral patch is associated with the shaded irregular face in Fig.5.3(b), and the 14 control vertices defining this patch are highlighted. Now an expression of the smooth limit surface can be easily formulated. Using Eqn.5.2, 5.3 and 5.4, it can be shown that

$$
\begin{aligned}
\mathbf{s} &= \sum_{i=1}^{m} \mathbf{J}_i \mathbf{p} + \sum_{j=1}^{n-m} \mathbf{J}_j \mathbf{p} \\
&= (\sum_{i=1}^{m} \mathbf{J}_i + \sum_{j=1}^{n-m} \mathbf{J}_j)\mathbf{p} \\
&= \mathbf{J}\mathbf{p},
\end{aligned}
\tag{5.5}
$$

where $\mathbf{J} = (\sum_{i=1}^{m} \mathbf{J}_i + \sum_{j=1}^{n-m} \mathbf{J}_j)$. Note that even though the initial mesh serves as the parametric domain of the smooth limit surface, each quadrilateral face in the initial mesh and consequently the smooth limit surface can be defined over a $[0, 1]^2$ domain.

5.2.2 Dynamics

The expression of the limit surface as given by Eqn.5.5 is same as the one derived in Chapter 3 (Eqn.3.15). However, the contents of the matrix $\mathbf{J}$ is totally different in two cases. Nevertheless, the dynamics of the limit surface can be formulated using the same symbolic expressions (which, when actually evaluated will lead to different expressions depending on the contents of the matrix $\mathbf{J}$). Therefore, the symbolic expression of the motion equation remains the same as in the earlier formulation of the dynamic Catmull-Clark subdivision surface model.

5.2.3 Finite Element Implementation

In the unified dynamic framework, the smooth limit surface obtained via Catmull-Clark subdivision process is expressed as a collection of quadrilateral patches. Each quadrilateral patch in the limit surface is considered as a finite element. Therefore, the limit surface under the unified framework consists of a single type of finite elements instead of two different types of elements as in Mandal et al. [57, 60] and Qin et al. [76]. The mass, damping and stiffness matrices for these elements along with the generalized force vector can be evaluated analytically, provided the material properties (like mass, damping, rigidity and bending distributions) have analytic expressions. These distribution functions are assumed to be constant in most cases. Now, the expressions of the mass, damping and stiffness matrices for a quadrilateral element which is a bicubic B-spline can be written as

$$\mathbf{M}_e = \int_0^1 \int_0^1 \mu \mathbf{J}_b^T \mathbf{J}_b \, du \, dv, \tag{5.6}$$

$$\mathbf{D}_e = \int_0^1 \int_0^1 \gamma \mathbf{J}_b^T \mathbf{J}_b \, du \, dv, \tag{5.7}$$

and

$$\begin{aligned}
\mathbf{K}_e = \int_0^1 \int_0^1 &(\alpha_{11}\{(\mathbf{J}_b)_u\}^T\{(\mathbf{J}_b)_u\} + \alpha_{22}\{(\mathbf{J}_b)_v\}^T\{(\mathbf{J}_b)_v\} + \beta_{11}\{(\mathbf{J}_b)_{uu}\}^T\{(\mathbf{J}_b)_{uu}\} \\
&+\beta_{12}\{(\mathbf{J}_b)_{uv}\}^T\{(\mathbf{J}_b)_{uv}\} + \beta_{22}\{(\mathbf{J}_b)_{vv}\}^T\{(\mathbf{J}_b)_{vv}\}) \, du \, dv
\end{aligned} \tag{5.8}$$

respectively, where $\mathbf{J}_b$ is the bicubic B-spline basis matrix, $\mu(u,v)$ is the mass density, $\gamma(u,v)$ is the damping density, $\alpha_{ii}(u,v)$ and $\beta_{ij}(u,v)$ are the tension and rigidity functions respectively. The subscript u and v denote partial derivatives with respect to u and v respectively. The subscript e is used to indicate elemental matrices which are of size $(16, 16)$. The expression for the corresponding generalized force vector is

$$\mathbf{f}_e = \int_0^1 \int_0^1 \mathbf{J}_b^T \mathbf{f}(u, v, t) du dv. \tag{5.9}$$

The mass, damping and stiffness matrices for the quadrilateral elements which are not bicubic B-splines (corresponding to the irregular faces) can be expressed analytically as well simply by replacing the matrix $\mathbf{J}_b$ in Eqn.5.6, 5.7 and 5.8 by the matrix $\mathbf{J}_{d_k}$ (refer to Eqn.5.4), where k denotes the degree of the extraordinary vertex associated with the corresponding irregular face. These elemental matrices are of size $(2k + 8, 2k + 8)$. The generalized force vector for these elements can also be determined in a similar fashion. It may be noted that the limits of integration need to be chosen carefully for elemental stiffness matrices as the second derivative diverges near the extraordinary points for Catmull-Clark subdivision surfaces. The elemental matrices combined together, either explicitly or implicitly, give the global matrices. Similarly, elemental generalized force vectors can be combined together to obtain the global generalized force vector. The motion equation is discretized and solved following similar techniques described in Chapter 3.

It may be noted that even though an analytical expression for a quadrilateral element in the limit surface which is not a bicubic B-spline exists, it is cumbersome to actually evaluate the elemental matrix expressions. Numerical integration using Gaussian quadrature may be used to obtain approximations of these elemental matrices. However, in this dissertation, an approach similar to the dynamic modified butterfly subdivision model presented in Chapter 4 is taken for implementation purposes. An approximation of the smooth limit surface is obtained by subdividing the initial control mesh j times, and a spring-mass system is developed on this j-th approximation level in a similar fashion as in Section 4.3. The physical matrices of this system are used as approximations to the actual physical matrices. These approximations have been found to be very efficient for implementation purposes.

5.3 Unified Dynamic Framework for Loop Subdivision Surfaces

Loop's subdivision scheme starts with a triangular control mesh and generates a smooth surface with triangular patches in the limit. It is an approximating subdivision scheme which generalizes recursive subdivision schemes for obtaining C^2 quartic triangular B-spline patches in a regular setting. In each step of Loop subdivision, each (non-boundary) triangular face is refined into 4 triangular faces using the following rules :

- For each (non-boundary) vertex V of degree n, a new vertex point is introduced. The position of this newly introduced vertex point is given by $\frac{\alpha(n)\mathbf{v}+\mathbf{v_1}+...+\mathbf{v_n}}{\alpha(n)+n}$, where $\mathbf{v}$ is the position vector of vertex V, $\mathbf{v_1},\ldots,\mathbf{v_n}$ are the vertex positions of the n vertices connected to vertex V, $\alpha(n) = \frac{n(1-\beta(n))}{\beta(n)}$ and $\beta(n) = \frac{5}{8} - \frac{(3+2cos(2\pi/n))^2}{64}$.

- For each (non-boundary) edge E, a new edge point is introduced. Let E be the connecting edge between vertices V_1 and V_2, and is shared by faces F_1 and F_2. If F_1 and F_2 have vertices V_{F_1} and V_{F_2} respectively (apart from V_1 and V_2), then the position of the newly introduced edge point is given by $\frac{3(\mathbf{v_1}+\mathbf{v_2})+\mathbf{v_{F_1}}+\mathbf{v_{F_2}}}{8}$,

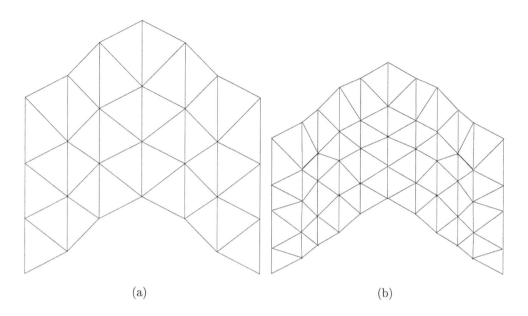

Figure 5.4. (a) The control polygon with triangular faces; (b) mesh obtained after one subdivision step using Loop's subdivision rules.

where $\mathbf{v_1}$, $\mathbf{v_2}$, $\mathbf{v_{F_1}}$ and $\mathbf{v_{F_2}}$ are the position vector of the vertex V_1, V_2, V_{F_1} and V_{F_2} respectively.

- New edges are formed by connecting each new vertex point to the new edge points corresponding to the edges incident on the old vertex, and by connecting each new edge point to the new edge points of the other edges in the two faces which shared the original edge.

- New faces are defined as faces enclosed by the new edges.

Examples of refining an initial mesh using Loop's subdivision rules are shown in Fig.5.4 and 5.5. These subdivision rules ensure tangent plane continuity of the limit surface even in a irregular setting, i.e., when the triangular control mesh has extraordinary vertices whose degree is not equal to 6. The limit surface shown in Fig.2.1(d) is actually obtained by subdividing the control mesh shown in Fig.2.1(a) using Loop subdivision rules. A detailed discussion on how to obtain positions and normals in the smooth limit surface generated by the Loop subdivision scheme can be found in Section 4.2 of Hoppe's thesis [39].

5.3.1 Local Parameterization

The limit surface obtained via Loop's subdivision scheme can be locally parameterized easily. This local parameterization scheme is very similar in nature to the one described for Catmull-Clark subdivision scheme in Section 5.2.1. For Loop's scheme, the smooth limit surface consists of triangular patches and the number of these triangular patches is same as the number of non-boundary triangular faces in the control mesh. Therefore, each of the triangular patch in the limit can be locally parameterized over the corresponding triangular face in the control mesh. In may be noted that each triangular face in the control mesh can be parameterized over a triangular domain whose vertices are located at $(0,0)$, $(0,1)$ and $(1,0)$, and hence each triangular patch and consequently the smooth limit surface can be defined over this domain (refer Fig.5.6).

The triangular patches in the smooth limit surface are of two types. For a non-boundary triangular face in the control mesh with no extraordinary vertices (i.e., with three vertices of degree 6), the corresponding triangular patch in the limit surface is a particular type of triangular B-spline (the three-direction quartic box spline) whose analytic expression is easy to obtain. This triangular B-spline patch is controlled by

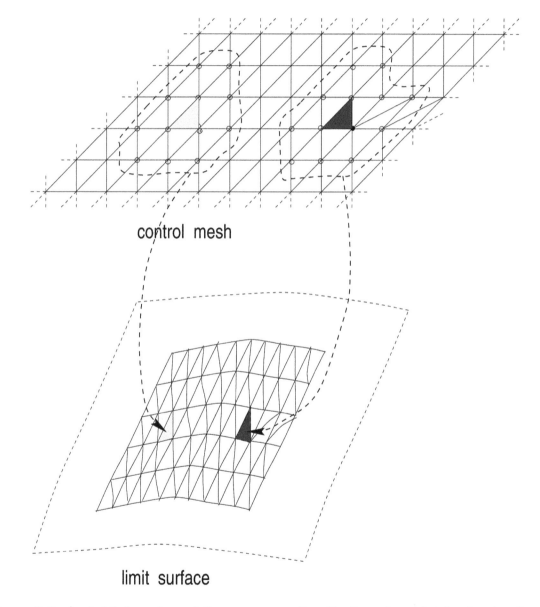

control mesh

limit surface

Figure 5.5. An initial mesh and the corresponding limit surface obtained using Loop's subdivision rules. The domains of the shaded triangular patches in the limit surface are the corresponding triangular faces in the initial mesh. The encircled vertices are the control vertices for the corresponding triangular patch in the limit surface.

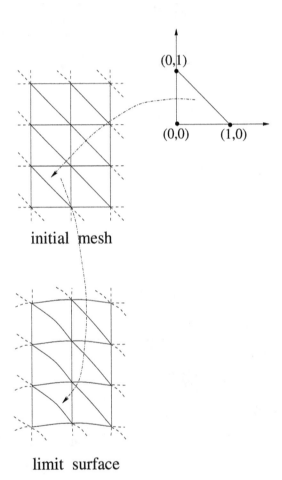

Figure 5.6. Each triangular patch in the limit surface can be associated with a non-boundary triangular face in the initial mesh, which in turn can be parameterized over a triangle with vertices at $(0,0)$, $(1,0)$ and $(0,1)$.

12 vertices as shown in Fig.5.5 (the set of enclosed vertices in the left hand side). The triangular patch in the limit surface corresponding to a non-boundary triangular face in the control mesh with one extraordinary vertex can also be expressed analytically using the schemes proposed by Stam [91]. This triangular patch is controlled by $n+6$ vertices in the control mesh where n is the degree of the extraordinary vertex. The set of control vertices for a triangular patch of the later type is shown in the right hand side of Fig.5.5. Therefore, each triangular patch in the limit surface can be expressed analytically, and an expression of the limit surface similar to Eqn.5.5 can be obtained.

5.3.2 Dynamics

Once an expression for the limit surface obtained via Loop's subdivision is obtained, the dynamic model can be developed following an exactly similar procedure described for Catmull-Clark subdivision scheme in Section 5.2.2. The motion equation of the dynamic Loop subdivision model can also be derived in a similar fashion.

5.3.3 Finite Element Implementation

The implementation of the dynamic framework for Loop subdivision scheme using the unified approach treats each triangular patch in the limit surface as a finite element. Each triangular patch has an analytic expression, and hence the elemental physical matrices and the generalized force vector can be derived analytically. The derivation of an exact expression for elemental matrices is cumbersome for the triangular patches corresponding to the triangular faces with an extraordinary vertex, and numerical integration using Gaussian quadrature may be used for deriving an approximation. However, a practical alternative for implementation is to subdivide the control mesh j times using Loop's subdivision rules, and to build a spring-mass system on this j-th level approximation as has been done for the dynamic modified butterfly subdivision model in Section 4.3. The physical matrices of this spring-mass system provide an approximation of the original physical matrices, and it works well in practice.

5.4 A General Outline of the Framework for Approximating Subdivision Schemes

The unified approach presented to provide a dynamic framework for Catmull-Clark and Loop subdivision schemes can be generalized easily. This approach involves three steps which are as follows :

1. The limit surface obtained via an approximating subdivision scheme can be expressed as a collection of smooth patches which can be locally parameterized over a corresponding face in the control mesh. Each patch is n-sided if it is locally parameterized over a n-sided face. Analytic expressions for each of these patches can be derived even in the presence of extraordinary vertices in the control mesh, and hence an expression of the limit surface can be obtained.

2. Once an expression of the limit surface is obtained, the dynamic framework can be developed by treating control vertex positions as a function of time. The corresponding motion equation can be derived.

3. Each patch in the limit surface is treated as a finite element in implementation. The elemental mass, damping and stiffness matrices along with the generalized force vector can be obtained by either analytic or numerical integration. Alternatively, the control mesh can be subdivided j times to obtain an approximation of the smooth limit surface, and a spring-mass system can be developed on this approximation mesh. The physical matrices of this system provide an approximation to the original physical matrices and works well in practice.

5.5   A General Outline of the Framework for Interpolatory Subdivision Schemes

Most of the interpolatory subdivision schemes are obtained by modifying the butterfly subdivision scheme [30]. Therefore, the framework developed for the modified butterfly subdivision scheme in Chapter 4 is pretty general and can be used for other interpolatory subdivision schemes as well. The only difference is that the basis functions as well as the set of control vertices for a patch in the limit surface depend on the chosen interpolatory subdivision rules. It may also be noted that unlike the approximating schemes, the physical matrices can not be obtained analytically as the basis functions corresponding to interpolatory subdivision schemes do not have any analytic expressions in general. Even though these matrices can be obtained via numerical integration, the spring-mass system developed in Chapter 4 is preferred for implementation purposes due to efficiency reasons.

CHAPTER 6
MULTIRESOLUTION DYNAMICS

The dynamic framework developed for subdivision surfaces allows the users to directly manipulate the smooth limit surface by applying synthesized forces. In any subdivision scheme, an initial (control) mesh is refined using specific subdivision rules to obtain a smooth surface in the limit. To develop the dynamic framework, this smooth limit surface is parameterized over the domain defined by the initial mesh and hence, the limit surface can be expressed as a function of the initial mesh. The users apply synthesized forces on the smooth limit surface which is transferred back on the initial mesh via a transformation matrix. The initial mesh evolves over time in response to the applied forces, and consequently the smooth limit surface deforms to obtain an equilibrium position where all forces are balanced. As noted earlier, even though various types of forces can be applied on the limit surface to obtain a desired effect, the possible shapes that can be obtained via evolution is directly related to the number of control vertices present in the initial mesh.

The concept of multilevel dynamics was introduced earlier in order to have varying number of control vertices in the initial mesh, and a wide range of shapes with arbitrary topology can be modeled within the dynamic framework. The reader is

104

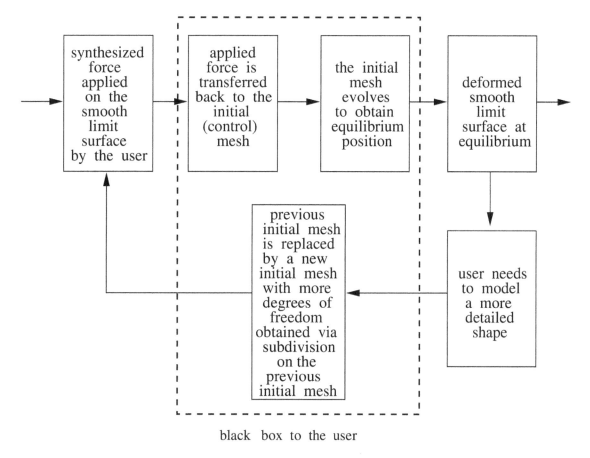

black box to the user

Figure 6.1. Schematic block diagram of the multilevel dynamics approach.

referred to Section 3.2.5 and Section 3.3.6 of this dissertation for the details of multi-level dynamics in the context of dynamic Catmull-Clark surfaces, and to Section 4.2.3 for the dynamic modified butterfly subdivision scheme. The concept of multilevel dynamics is illustrated with block diagrams in Fig.6.1. This multilevel dynamics can be considered as a subdivision surface-based coarse-to-fine modeling framework and can be summarized as follows. The user starts with a smooth limit surface which has a very simple initial mesh with few control vertices. This smooth surface is deformed by applying synthesized forces so that the limit surface at equilibrium would look like the final desired shape but without the details in it. Then, the number of control vertices in the initial mesh is increased by replacing the initial mesh at equilibrium by another one obtained via one subdivision step on the old initial mesh, and the old initial mesh is discarded. Both of these old and new initial mesh represent the same limit surface, but the latter has more control vertices. Now, this new initial mesh, and consequently the smooth limit surface, can be deformed to obtain a shape at equilibrium which has more details. This process is repeated till the deformed smooth surface has all the desired details.

The limitation of the multilevel dynamics approach is that once a finer resolution is chosen, the modeler can not opt for a lower resolution as the dynamics is defined on the current initial mesh. There is no way of having the dynamics defined on a simpler initial mesh, at the same time preserving the already obtained details in the model within the multilevel dynamics approach. This is potentially a severe restriction. For example, let us imagine the scenario depicted in Fig.6.2. The modeler has recovered

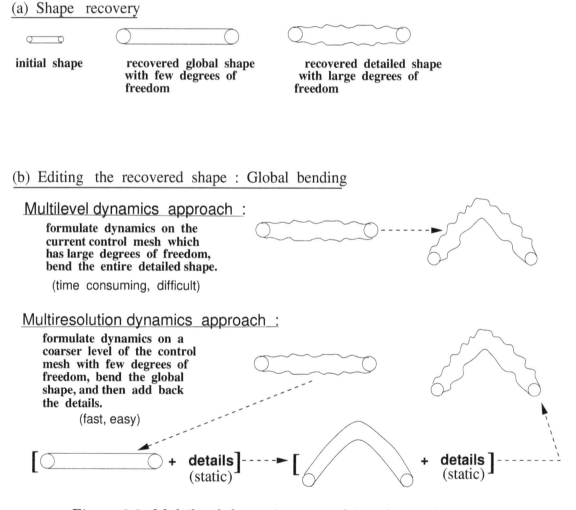

(a) Shape recovery

initial shape

recovered global shape
with few degrees of
freedom

recovered detailed shape
with large degrees of
freedom

(b) Editing the recovered shape : Global bending

Multilevel dynamics approach :

formulate dynamics on the
current control mesh which
has large degrees of freedom,
bend the entire detailed shape.

(time consuming, difficult)

Multiresolution dynamics approach :

formulate dynamics on a
coarser level of the control
mesh with few degrees of
freedom, bend the global
shape, and then add back
the details.

(fast, easy)

[⬭ + **details**] ----▶ [/\ + **details**]
(static)   (static)

Figure 6.2. Multilevel dynamics vs. multiresolution dynamics.

a long straight pipe-like shape with lots of detail by synthesized force application on a smooth limit surface. This smooth limit surface initially had a simple initial mesh with few vertices, but the current initial mesh after many model subdivision steps has large number of control vertices. Now, if the modeler wants to bend this straight pipe-like shape, the synthesized forces applied on the smooth limit surface need to deform an initial mesh with a large number of control vertices. It would have been much easier and faster if a lower resolution version of the current initial mesh could be deformed with the details being added back when the shape has bent to the desired extent in response to the applied synthesized forces. Also, it has been pointed out in Section 2.5 that the dynamic framework can integrate shape recovery and shape modeling in a unified framework where the recovered shape can easily be edited as well. However, if the modeler wants a global change in the recovered shape, a lower resolution control mesh (than the one obtained via shape recovery process) may be required, and the details need to be preserved at the same time.

A multiresolution representation of the initial mesh is proposed in this chapter to solve the above-mentioned problem. At equilibrium, an initial mesh is subdivided to obtain an initial mesh with more control vertices (degrees of freedom). Instead of developing the dynamics on this newly obtained initial mesh as in the multilevel dynamics approach, the dynamics is developed on a representation which views the newly obtained initial mesh as the previous initial mesh plus detail (wavelet) coefficients needed to get the current initial mesh (see Fig.6.3). This is essentially developing the dynamics on a multiresolution representation of the evolving initial

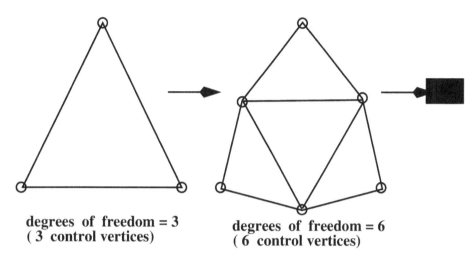

degrees of freedom = 3
(3 control vertices)

degrees of freedom = 6
(6 control vertices)

(a) Multilevel approach

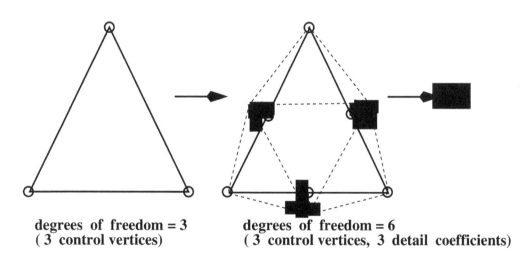

degrees of freedom = 3
(3 control vertices)

degrees of freedom = 6
(3 control vertices, 3 detail coefficients)

(b) Multiresolution approach

Figure 6.3. Representation of the degrees of freedom in multilevel dynamics and multiresolution dynamics approach.

mesh which has undergone model subdivision step(s) to increase the degrees of freedom. It may be noted that both the multilevel and the multiresolution approach have same degrees of freedom to represent the initial mesh obtained after a model subdivision step, but the degrees of freedom for the multilevel dynamics approach are the control vertex positions in the newly obtained mesh whereas, the degrees of freedom for the current approach are the control vertex positions in the previous initial mesh and the detailed coefficients necessary to obtain the current initial mesh from the previous one. The multiresolution approach has the benefit that the modeler can opt for a lower resolution initial mesh later, on which the dynamics can be defined, at the same time preserving the detailed coefficients of the initial mesh on which the dynamics is currently defined. This concept will be detailed further in later sections, but first an overview of the multiresolution analysis is provided so that the reader can easily follow the rest of the material presented in this chapter.

<u>6.1   Overview of Multiresolution Analysis and Wavelets</u>

The basic idea of multiresolution analysis is to decompose a complicated function into a lower resolution version along with a set of detailed coefficients (also known as wavelet coefficients) necessary to recover the original function. Multiresolution analysis and wavelets have widespread applications in diverse areas like signal analysis [55, 81], image processing [26, 56], physics [2], numerical analysis [7], computer vision [48] and computer graphics [6, 13, 16, 17, 31, 32, 35, 45, 50, 53, 67, 68, 70, 85, 86, 104, 110]. The specific areas in computer graphics that involve multiresolution analysis and wavelets include, but not limited to, global illumination [16, 17, 35, 85], curve, mesh and image editing [6, 32, 110], video processing [31], surface viewing [13],

surface interpolation [70], creating surfaces from contours [67, 68], animation control

[50], polyhedral compression [53], modeling [45, 104] and representing functions on

a sphere [86]. Various applications of wavelets in computer graphics are detailed in

Stollnitz et al. [92]. The idea of multiresolution analysis is explained next with a

simple example.

Let $\mathbf{p}^j$ be a vector containing functional values of some arbitrary function at n

discrete points. A lower resolution representation of the function using m $(m < n)$

functional values can be obtained from $\mathbf{p}^j$ by doing certain weighted averages of the

n functional values stored in $\mathbf{p}^j$. This is essentially a low pass filtering followed by

down-sampling, and the entire operation can be expressed as

$$\mathbf{p}^{j-1} = \mathbf{A}^j \mathbf{p}^j, \tag{6.1}$$

where $\mathbf{p}^{j-1}$ is the m-valued vector representing a lower resolution version and the

matrix $\mathbf{A}^j$ is of size (m, n) and implements the low pass filter along with the down-

sampler.

The lower resolution $\mathbf{p}^{j-1}$ has fewer functional values than $\mathbf{p}^j$, and hence some

amount of detail present in $\mathbf{p}^j$ is lost due to the low pass filtering process. If the low

pass filter $\mathbf{A}^j$ is chosen appropriately, it is possible to capture the lost detail by high

pass filtering followed by a down-sampling of the original functional values stored in

$\mathbf{p}^j$. This operation can be expressed as

$$\mathbf{q}^{j-1} = \mathbf{B}^j \mathbf{p}^j, \tag{6.2}$$

where $\mathbf{q}^{j-1}$ is a $(n-m)$-valued vector representing detailed coefficients necessary to recover $\mathbf{p}^j$ from $\mathbf{p}^{j-1}$. The matrix $\mathbf{B}^j$ is of size $(n-m,n)$ and implements the high pass filter along with the down-sampler. The high pass filter $\mathbf{B}^j$ is related to the low pass filter $\mathbf{A}^j$. These two filters, $\mathbf{A}^j$ and $\mathbf{B}^j$, are known as *analysis filters* and the process of splitting a high resolution vector $\mathbf{p}^j$ into a low resolution vector $\mathbf{p}^{j-1}$ and a vector $\mathbf{q}^{j-1}$ storing detail coefficients is known as *decomposition*.

The original vector $\mathbf{p}^j$ can be reconstructed from the vectors $\mathbf{p}^{j-1}$ and $\mathbf{q}^{j-1}$ if the synthesis filters are chosen correctly. This is called the *reconstruction* process, which can be expressed as

$$\mathbf{p}^j = \mathbf{P}^j \mathbf{p}^{j-1} + \mathbf{Q}^j \mathbf{q}^{j-1}, \tag{6.3}$$

where $\mathbf{P}^j$ is a refinement matrix of size (n,m) and $\mathbf{Q}^j$ is a perturbation matrix of size $(n, m-n)$. The refinement matrix $\mathbf{P}^j$ encodes the rules for obtaining a vector of larger size from a given vector and the perturbation matrix $\mathbf{Q}^j$ encodes how to obtain a perturbation of $(\mathbf{p}^j - \mathbf{P}^j \mathbf{p}^{j-1})$ from the given detailed coefficient vector $\mathbf{q}^{j-1}$. The matrices $\mathbf{P}^j$ and $\mathbf{Q}^j$ are collectively called *synthesis filters*, and are related to the analysis filters.

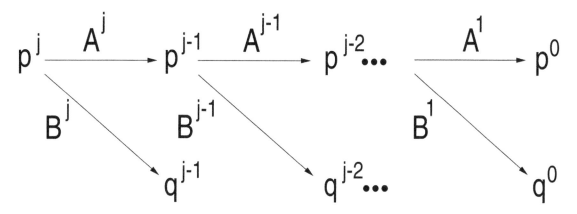

Figure 6.4. The filter bank.

The process of decomposition can be continued recursively. For example, $\mathbf{p}^j$ is decomposed into a lower resolution part $\mathbf{p}^{j-1}$ and a detail part $\mathbf{q}^{j-1}$. Then, $\mathbf{p}^{j-1}$ can be expressed as a lower resolution part $\mathbf{p}^{j-2}$ and another detail part $\mathbf{q}^{j-2}$. This recursive process is depicted in Fig.6.4 and is known as *filter bank*. The original vector is decomposed into a hierarchy of lower resolution parts $\mathbf{p}^{j-1}, \mathbf{p}^{j-2}, \ldots, \mathbf{p}^0$ and detail parts $\mathbf{q}^{j-1}, \mathbf{q}^{j-2}, \ldots, \mathbf{q}^0$. The original vector $\mathbf{p}^j$ can be recovered from the sequence $\mathbf{p}^0, \mathbf{q}^0, \mathbf{q}^1, \ldots, \mathbf{q}^{j-2}, \mathbf{q}^{j-1}$. This sequence has the same size as that of the original vector and is known as the *wavelet transform* of the original vector.

The analysis and synthesis filters are designed in such a fashion that the low resolution versions are good approximations of the original function in a least square sense. The decomposition and reconstruction processes should have time complexity $O(n)$, where n is the size of the vector being decomposed or reconstructed. A detail (wavelet) coefficient value should also be related to the error introduced in the approximation when that particular coefficient is set to zero.

Multiresolution analysis is a framework for developing these analysis and synthesis filters. It involves derivation of a sequence of nested linear spaces $V^0 \subset V^1 \subset V^2 \subset \ldots$ such that the resolution of the functions contained in some space V^j increases with increasing j. Also, there exists an orthogonal complement space W^{j-1} for each V^{j-1}, $j = 1, 2, \ldots$ such that $V^{j-1} \oplus W^{j-1} = V^j$, i.e., the linear space V^{j-1} and its orthogonal complement space W^{j-1} together span the linear space V^j. The inner product between any two functions at some level j, $j = 0, 1, 2, \ldots$ needs to be defined in order to derive the orthogonal complement space.

Let ϕ_1^j, ϕ_2^j, $\ldots$, ϕ_n^j be a set of basis functions spanning the linear space V^j. These basis functions are also called *scaling functions* for level j. Now, $V^{j-1} \subset V^j$ and hence the basis functions ϕ_1^{j-1}, ϕ_2^{j-1}, $\ldots$, ϕ_m^{j-1}, spanning the linear space V^{j-1}, can be expressed as a linear combination of the basis functions than span the linear space V^j. This refinability of scaling functions is used to construct the refinement matrix $\mathbf{P}^j$, which should satisfy the expression

$$\mathbf{\Phi}^{j-1} = \mathbf{\Phi}^j \mathbf{P}^j, \tag{6.4}$$

where $\mathbf{\Phi}^{j-1} = [\phi_1^{j-1}, \phi_2^{j-1}, \ldots, \phi_m^{j-1}]$, $\mathbf{\Phi}^j = [\phi_1^j, \phi_2^j, \ldots, \phi_n^j]$, and $\mathbf{P}^j$ is the (n, m) refinement matrix introduced earlier (Eqn.6.3). Similarly, let ψ_1^{j-1}, ψ_2^{j-1}, $\ldots$, ψ_{n-m}^{j-1} be a set of basis functions that span the linear space W^{j-1}. These basis functions, also known as *wavelets* at level $j - 1$, together with the basis functions of linear space V^{j-1} form a basis for the linear space V^j. Next, the perturbation matrix $\mathbf{Q}^j$ can be constructed such that it satisfies the expression

$$\mathbf{\Psi}^{j-1} = \mathbf{\Phi}^j \mathbf{Q}^j, \tag{6.5}$$

where $\mathbf{\Psi}^{j-1} = [\psi_1^{j-1}, \psi_2^{j-1}, \ldots, \psi_{n-m}^{j-1}]$, and $\mathbf{Q}^j$ is the $(n, n-m)$ perturbation matrix introduced in Eqn.6.3. A more compact expression may be obtained by combining Eqn.6.4 and 6.5, which can be written as

$$[\mathbf{\Phi}^{j-1} \mid \mathbf{\Psi}^{j-1}] \quad = \quad \mathbf{\Phi}^j \ [\mathbf{P}^j \mid \mathbf{Q}^j]. \tag{6.6}$$

The analysis filters $\mathbf{A}^j$ and $\mathbf{B}^j$ should satisfy the inverse relation

$$[\mathbf{\Phi}^{j-1} \mid \mathbf{\Psi}^{j-1}] \ \begin{bmatrix} \mathbf{A}^j \\ \hline \mathbf{B}^j \end{bmatrix} \quad = \quad \mathbf{\Phi}^j. \tag{6.7}$$

Both the matrices $[\mathbf{P}^j \mid \mathbf{Q}^j]$ and $\left[\frac{\mathbf{A}^j}{\mathbf{B}^j}\right]$ are of size (n, n) and satisfy the relation

$$[\mathbf{P}^j \mid \mathbf{Q}^j] \quad = \quad \begin{bmatrix} \mathbf{A}^j \\ \hline \mathbf{B}^j \end{bmatrix}^{-1}. \tag{6.8}$$

6.2 Multiresolution Analysis for Surfaces of Arbitrary Topology

Classically, the multiresolution analysis was developed on infinite domains such as real line $\Re$ and plane $\Re^2$ [22, 23]. Infinite domains are spatially invariant and hence a single basis function at the coarsest resolution can be dilated and translated to form the basis functions at higher resolutions. However, many applications need multiresolution analysis on bounded intervals and techniques for imposing boundary constrains have also been derived [19, 79]. The idea of generalizing multiresolution analysis on arbitrary manifolds was first introduced by Lounsbery et al. [52, 53], and was further improved by Stollnitz et al. [92] using the concepts of *lifting scheme* [93]. In this dissertation, the multiresolution schemes derived by Stollnitz et al. [92] for surfaces of arbitrary topology will be adopted to develop the multiresolution dynamic framework for subdivision surfaces.

Multiresolution analysis using wavelets can be categorized into three types - orthogonal [22, 55], semiorthogonal [18] and biorthogonal [20, 93]. A multiresolution scheme has orthogonal wavelets if the wavelets are orthogonal to one another, and every wavelet is orthogonal to every coarser scaling function. It is difficult to construct orthogonal wavelets that have local support (i.e., non-zero over a small section of the domain). Locally supported wavelets are important as they lead to sparse synthesis and analysis filters which in turn lead to linear time complexity in vector size. Wavelets with local support can be constructed by relaxing the orthogonality constraint. If the wavelets are orthogonal to each other within one resolution but not across different resolutions, then they are called semiorthogonal wavelets. In a biorthogonal setting, the orthogonality constraint is dropped where W^{j-1} is some (and not orthogonal) complement of V^{j-1} in V^j. The wavelets on arbitrary manifolds developed by Stollnitz et al. [92] and used in this dissertation are biorthogonal. The multiresolution analysis on arbitrary manifolds involve (1) developing nested spaces using subdivision schemes, (2) selecting an inner product on arbitrary manifold and (3) constructing biorthogonal wavelets, which are discussed in the rest of this section.

It may be noted that there is a slight deviation from the standard notational convention of writing vectors in bold face lower case and matrices in bold face upper case letters in a particular situation in the rest of this chapter. The collection of control point positions are assumed to be a three-column matrix (one for each of the x, y and z components) instead of a vector whose size is thrice the number of control points. Consequently, the three-row matrix representing the collection of basis functions becomes a row vector. This approach is more natural for developing the wavelet expressions, whereas the opposite was true for the theory developed in earlier chapters. However, bold face lower case letters are used to represent the three-column matrix of control vertex positions and bold face upper case letters are used to represent the vector of basis functions, so that the reader does not get confused with a new notation for representing the same thing in a different format. The notational purity is given away to a small extent for the sake of clarity. All the expressions can be reformulated by merging the columns of the three-column matrix into a single vector, but the resulting expressions will unnecessarily obscure the intuitiveness contained in the current set of expressions.

6.2.1 Nested Spaces through Subdivision

In previous chapters, it has been shown that the smooth limit surface generated by a recursive subdivision scheme in general can be written as

$$\mathbf{s}(\mathbf{x}) = \mathbf{J}(\mathbf{x})\mathbf{p}, \qquad (6.9)$$

where $\mathbf{s}$ is the smooth limit surface, $\mathbf{J}$ is a collection of basis functions spanning the space defined by the control mesh S, $\mathbf{p}$ is the vertex positions in the control mesh and $x \in S$. A general outline on how to obtain this expression for any type of subdivision scheme has been provided in Section 5.4 and 5.5 of this dissertation and specific examples can be found in Eqn.3.15 and Eqn.5.5 for Catmull-Clark subdivision scheme and in Eqn.4.11 for the modified butterfly scheme.

Let the control mesh defining the smooth limit surface be S^0. Renaming the control vertex vector $\mathbf{p}$ to $\mathbf{p}^0$ and the basis (scaling) function matrix $\mathbf{J}$ to $\mathbf{J}^0$, Eqn.6.9 can be rewritten as

$$\mathbf{s}(\mathbf{x}) = \mathbf{J}^0(\mathbf{x})\mathbf{p}^0, \qquad (6.10)$$

where $x \in S^0$. Let S^1 be a mesh obtained by subdividing S^0 once using the subdivision rules. If the control vertices of the mesh S^1 are collected in a vector $\mathbf{p}^1$, then

$$\mathbf{p}^1 = \mathbf{P}^1\mathbf{p}^0, \qquad (6.11)$$

where $\mathbf{P}^1$ is the subdivision (refinement) matrix. However, the control mesh S^1 has the same limit surface (as it is obtained via one subdivision step on the control mesh S^0) and hence the same limit surface can be written as

$$
\begin{aligned}
\mathbf{s}(\mathbf{x}) &= \mathbf{J}^1(\mathbf{x})\mathbf{p}^1 \\
&= \mathbf{J}^1(\mathbf{x})\mathbf{P}^1\mathbf{p}^0, \qquad (6.12)
\end{aligned}
$$

where J^1 is a collection of basis (scaling) functions spanning the space defined by S^1.

From Eqn.6.10 and Eqn.6.12, it is obvious that

$$\mathbf{J}^0(\mathbf{x}) = \mathbf{J}^1(\mathbf{x})\mathbf{P}^1, \tag{6.13}$$

which essentially means that the scaling functions at subdivision level 0 can be expressed as a linear combination of the scaling functions at subdivision level 1, i.e., $V^0(S^0) \subset V^1(S^0)$. This can be generalized for other subdivision levels as well, and hence subdivision naturally leads to a nested space sequence $V^0(S^0) \subset V^1(S^0) \subset V^2(S^0) \subset \ldots$ which will be utilized for multiresolution analysis on arbitrary manifolds.

6.2.2 Inner Product

The inner product proposed in Stollnitz et al. [92] is used in this dissertation. If f_a and f_b are two functions defined on the domain S^0, then their inner product $< f_a, f_b >$ is given by

$$< f_a, f_b > = \sum_{\gamma \in F(S^0)} \frac{1}{a(\gamma)} \int_{\mathbf{x} \in \gamma} f_a(\mathbf{x}) f_b(\mathbf{x}) d\mathbf{x}, \tag{6.14}$$

where $F(S^0)$ is the set of (triangular or quadrilateral, depending on the subdivision scheme) faces in the control mesh S^0, γ is a face in the set $F(S^0)$, $a(\gamma)$ is the area of the face γ and $d\mathbf{x}$ is the usual differential area in $\Re^3$.

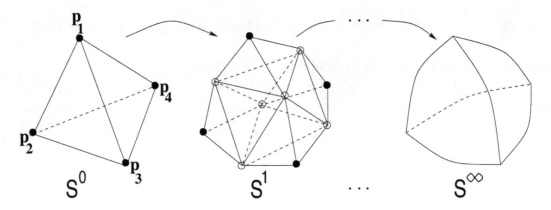

Figure 6.5. Subdivision refinement of a tetrahedron.

6.2.3   Biorthogonal Surface Wavelets on Arbitrary Manifold

The biorthogonal wavelets discussed here can be developed for any subdivision scheme in general. However, some minor modifications are needed in some situations. The construction is based on the lifting scheme [93] where first "lazy" wavelets at level $j - 1$ are constructed using some scaling functions at level j, and then these wavelets are "lifted" so that they become as orthogonal as desired to the scaling functions at level $j - 1$. These concepts are described below using a simple example. A more detailed discussion on this construction can be found in Stollnitz et al. [92].

Let S^0, as shown in Fig.6.5, be a (tetrahedral) control mesh which when refined using some subdivision rules leads to a smooth surface in the limit. The subdivision rules refine each triangular face into four triangular faces by introducing new vertices corresponding to each edge in the mesh as shown in Fig.6.5. Let the smooth surface in the limit be $\mathbf{s}$ (denoted by S^∞ in Fig.6.5). Let $\mathbf{p}^0$ be the collection of four control vertex positions defining the control mesh S^0. Now, there exists scaling functions $\phi_i^0(\mathbf{x})$, $\mathbf{x} \in S^0$, associated with each vertex $\mathbf{p}_i$, $i = 1, \ldots, 4$, such that they span the space $V^0(S^0)$. These scaling functions depend on the subdivision scheme involved and may or may not have analytic expressions. These scaling functions are collected in $\mathbf{J}^0(\mathbf{x}) = [\phi_1^0(\mathbf{x}), \phi_2^0(\mathbf{x}), \phi_3^0(\mathbf{x}), \phi_4^0(\mathbf{x})]$. The smooth limit surface $\mathbf{s}$ can be written as

$$\mathbf{s} = \mathbf{J}^0(\mathbf{x})\, \mathbf{p}^0, \tag{6.15}$$

where $\mathbf{x} \in S^0$. The control mesh S^1 is obtained by subdividing the control mesh S^0 once. The ten control vertices of the mesh S^1 can be categorized into two classes : (1) four control vertices corresponding to the four control vertices in original mesh S^0 (the filled dots in Fig.6.5) and (2) six control vertices corresponding to the six edges in original mesh S^0 (the unfilled dots in Fig.6.5). If the control vertex positions of the mesh S^1 are collected in $\mathbf{p}^1$ such that the "old" vertices corresponding to the vertices in the original mesh precede the "new" vertices corresponding to the edges in the original mesh, then

$$\mathbf{p}^1 = \mathbf{P}^1 \mathbf{p}^0 = \begin{bmatrix} \mathbf{P}^1_{old} \\ \\ \mathbf{P}^1_{new} \end{bmatrix} \mathbf{p}^0, \tag{6.16}$$

where $\mathbf{P}^1$ is the subdivision matrix, and $\mathbf{P}^1_{old}$ and $\mathbf{P}^1_{new}$ are portions of the subdivision matrix that encode rules to obtain the "old" and "new" vertices respectively. Basis functions corresponding to the vertices in $\mathbf{p}^1$ can be collected in $\mathbf{J}^1(x) = [\mathbf{J}^1_{old}(x) \mid \mathbf{J}^1_{new}(x)] = [\phi_1^1(\mathbf{x}), \ldots, \phi_4^1(\mathbf{x}) \mid \phi_5^1(\mathbf{x}), \ldots, \phi_{10}^1(\mathbf{x})]$, where the first four basis functions are associated with old vertices and the last six basis functions are associated with new vertices. The same smooth limit surface **s** can be written as

$$\mathbf{s} = \mathbf{J}^1(\mathbf{x})\, \mathbf{p}^1. \tag{6.17}$$

Evidently, the dimension of $V^0(S^0)$ and $V^1(S^0)$ are 4 and 10 respectively. In the lazy wavelet construction, a complement space $W^0(S^0)$ of dimension 6 is constructed with the set of basis functions corresponding to the new vertices in S^1, i.e., the wavelets spanning $W^0(S^0)$ are $\mathbf{W}^0(\mathbf{x}) = [\psi_1^0(\mathbf{x}), \ldots, \psi_6^0(\mathbf{x})] = [\phi_5^1(\mathbf{x}), \ldots, \phi_{10}^1(\mathbf{x})]$. This construction is called "lazy" because no extra computation need to be done to derive the wavelets. The refinement relations for the lazy wavelet construction can be compactly written as

$$[\mathbf{J}^0(\mathbf{x}) \mid \mathbf{W}^0(\mathbf{x})] = [\mathbf{J}_{old}^1(x) \mid \mathbf{J}_{new}^1(x)]\,[\mathbf{P}_{lazy}^1 \mid \mathbf{Q}_{lazy}^1], \tag{6.18}$$

where $\mathbf{P}_{lazy}^1 = \mathbf{P}^1$ and

$$[\mathbf{P}_{lazy}^1 \mid \mathbf{Q}_{lazy}^1] = \begin{bmatrix} \mathbf{P}_{old}^1 & \mathbf{0} \\ \mathbf{P}_{new}^1 & \mathbf{I} \end{bmatrix},$$

0 and **I** denoting zero and identity matrix respectively. After developing the synthesis filters for the lazy wavelets, the analysis filters can be derived using the inverse relation and are given by

$$\left[\frac{\mathbf{A}_{lazy}^1}{\mathbf{B}_{lazy}^1}\right] = \left[\begin{array}{cc} \mathbf{P}_{old}^1 & \mathbf{0} \\ \mathbf{P}_{new}^1 & \mathbf{I} \end{array}\right]^{-1} = \left[\begin{array}{cc} \left(\mathbf{P}_{old}^1\right)^{-1} & \mathbf{0} \\ -\mathbf{P}_{new}^1\left(\mathbf{P}_{old}^1\right)^{-1} & \mathbf{I} \end{array}\right]. \qquad (6.19)$$

The lazy wavelet construction developed here can be generalized for any subdivision level j in a straight-forward manner. The synthesis and analysis filters at level j for a subdivision scheme can be written as

$$[\mathbf{P}_{lazy}^j \mid \mathbf{Q}_{lazy}^j] = \left[\begin{array}{cc} \mathbf{P}_{old}^j & \mathbf{0} \\ \mathbf{P}_{new}^j & \mathbf{I} \end{array}\right], \qquad (6.20)$$

and

$$\left[\frac{\mathbf{A}_{lazy}^j}{\mathbf{B}_{lazy}^j}\right] = \left[\begin{array}{cc} \mathbf{P}_{old}^j & \mathbf{0} \\ \mathbf{P}_{new}^j & \mathbf{I} \end{array}\right]^{-1} = \left[\begin{array}{cc} \left(\mathbf{P}_{old}^j\right)^{-1} & \mathbf{0} \\ -\mathbf{P}_{new}^j\left(\mathbf{P}_{old}^j\right)^{-1} & \mathbf{I} \end{array}\right], \qquad (6.21)$$

respectively, where $\mathbf{P}_{old}^j$ encodes subdivision rules for obtaining "old" vertices at j-th level corresponding to the vertices in the $(j-1)$-th level control mesh and $\mathbf{P}_{new}^j$ encodes rules for obtaining the other "new" vertices in the j-th level control mesh.

It may be noted that the lazy wavelet construction leads to sparse synthesis matrices. However, the corresponding analysis filters may not be sparse in general as inverse of $\mathbf{P}_{old}^j$ is not necessarily sparse. This implies that even though the synthesis can be done in linear time with respect to the number of vertices, the complexity of the analysis depends on how fast the inverse can be computed. The synthesis can not be done in linear time in case of approximating subdivision schemes. However, $\mathbf{P}_{old}^j$

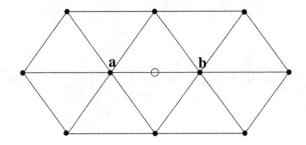

Wavelet associated with the edge
connecting **a** and **b**

Lazy : the scaling function associated with
the introduced vertex at higher level

Lifted : the scaling function associated with
the introduced vertex at higher level
- (weighted combination of the scaling
functions associated with the solid
vertices)

Figure 6.6. Wavelet construction.

is an identity matrix for interpolatory subdivision schemes, and hence both synthesis

and analysis can be done in linear time for interpolatory subdivision schemes. The

simplified expressions of the synthesis and analysis filters in case of interpolatory

subdivision scheme are given by

$$[\mathbf{P}^j_{lazy} \mid \mathbf{Q}^j_{lazy}] = \begin{bmatrix} \mathbf{I} & \mathbf{0} \\ \mathbf{P}^j_{new} & \mathbf{I} \end{bmatrix},$$
(6.22)

and

$$\begin{bmatrix} \mathbf{A}^j_{lazy} \\ \hline \mathbf{B}^j_{lazy} \end{bmatrix} = \begin{bmatrix} \mathbf{I} & \mathbf{0} \\ -\mathbf{P}^j_{new} & \mathbf{I} \end{bmatrix},$$
(6.23)

respectively.

The lazy wavelets are easy to construct. However, a lower resolution mesh obtained using the analysis filters of the lazy wavelet construction is far from the least-squares-best approximation. Lazy wavelets at some level $(j-1)$ are nowhere orthogonal to V^{j-1}. The lifting scheme [93] improves the lazy wavelets at level $(j-1)$ by subtracting a liner combination of the coarser level scaling functions which overlap to a given wavelet. The resulting wavelet function becomes somewhat more orthogonal to the coarser level scaling functions than the original lazy wavelet. Mathematically, a "lifted" wavelet at level $(j-1)$ can be expressed as

$$
\begin{aligned}
\psi_{lift,i}^{j-1}(\mathbf{x}) &= \psi_{lazy,i}^{j-1}(\mathbf{x}) - \sum_l s_{l,i}^j \phi_l^{j-1}(\mathbf{x}) \\
&= \phi_{new,i}^j(\mathbf{x}) - \sum_l s_{l,i}^j \phi_l^{j-1}(\mathbf{x}),
\end{aligned}
\tag{6.24}
$$

where i-th lazy wavelet function at level $(j-1)$ is the scaling function associated with the i-th "new" vertex at level j, and l is restricted to a few vertices at level $(j-1)$ in the neighborhood of the i-th new vertex at level j (Fig.6.6). In order to get the values of $s_{l,i}^j$ for the lifted wavelet i, a linear system of equations is derived and solved in a least squares sense by imposing the constraints $< \psi_{lift,i}^{j-1}(\mathbf{x}), \phi_k^{j-1}(\mathbf{x}) > = 0$ for all k, such that the supports of $\psi_{lift,i}^{j-1}(\mathbf{x})$ and $\phi_k^{j-1}(\mathbf{x})$ overlap. The number of non-zero entries is in $s_{l,i}^j$ needs to be controlled. A large number of non-zero entries will lead to a lifted wavelet function that is nearly orthogonal to the coarser level scaling functions, at the same time the multiresolution analysis will become more time consuming, and hence a tradeoff needs to be decided as far as orthogonality and time of computation is concerned. In Stollnitz et al. [92], "k-disk wavelets" are constructed for triangular mesh-based subdivision schemes where the non-zero entries of $s_{l,i}^j$ are restricted to the vertices at level $(j-1)$ which are within the k-neighborhood of the i-th "new" vertex at level j. The reader is referred to Stollnitz et al. [92] for the details of the construction. Once the non-zero values of $s_{l,i}^j$ are computed, they can be assembled to a matrix $\mathbf{S}^j$. Then, the expressions for the synthesis and analysis filters of the lifted wavelet scheme can be written as

$$[\mathbf{P}_{lift}^j \mid \mathbf{Q}_{lift}^j] \;=\; [\mathbf{P}_{lazy}^j \mid \mathbf{Q}_{lazy}^j - P_{lazy}^j \mathbf{S}^j], \tag{6.25}$$

and

$$\begin{bmatrix} \mathbf{A}_{lift}^j \\ \hline \mathbf{B}_{lift}^j \end{bmatrix} \;=\; \begin{bmatrix} \mathbf{A}_{lazy}^j + \mathbf{S}^j \mathbf{B}_{lazy}^j \\ \hline \mathbf{B}_{lazy}^j \end{bmatrix}, \tag{6.26}$$

respectively.

6.3 Multiresolution Representation

The multiresolution analysis on arbitrary manifold was developed to obtain good low resolution approximations of complicated meshes. This is a top-down technique where one starts with a complicated arbitrary topology mesh and goes on obtaining lower resolution meshes using analysis filters. The complicated mesh on which multiresolution analysis is applied can be reconstructed using the synthesis filters. In this dissertation, the multiresolution technique is used in a novel bottom-up approach where an evolving control mesh of a dynamic subdivision surface is subdivided at equilibrium to obtain more degrees of freedom, and then, the resulting control mesh is treated as the previous control mesh and a collection of detail (wavelet) coefficients.

Of course, the detail coefficients are zero when an control mesh is replaced by another control mesh obtained by a pure subdivision step on the previous mesh, but becomes non-zero as the new control mesh (represented as previous control mesh and wavelet coefficients) evolves over time in response with the synthesized force application. This idea is further illustrated in the rest of this section.

Let $\mathbf{s}$ be a smooth limit surface obtained via infinite number of subdivision steps on an initial mesh S^0, whose vertex positions are collected in $\mathbf{p}^0$. As mentioned earlier, the limit surface can be written as

$$\mathbf{s} = \mathbf{J}^0 \mathbf{p}^0, \tag{6.27}$$

where $\mathbf{J}^0$ is a collection of basis functions. If the control mesh S^1 is obtained by subdividing S^0 once, then the same limit surface can be expressed as

$$\mathbf{s} = \mathbf{J}^1 \mathbf{p}^1, \tag{6.28}$$

where $\mathbf{p}^1$ is the collection of vertex positions of the mesh S^1 and $\mathbf{J}^1$ is the collection of corresponding basis functions. Since $\mathbf{p}^1 = \mathbf{P}^1 \mathbf{p}^0$, the limit surface $\mathbf{s}$ can also be written as

$$\mathbf{s} = \mathbf{J}^1 \mathbf{P}^1 \mathbf{p}^0. \tag{6.29}$$

The difference between Eqn.6.27 and Eqn.6.28 is that the limit surface $\mathbf{s}$ has more degrees of freedom (control vertices) for representation in the latter in comparison with the former. However, in Eqn.6.29, even though the limit surface is expressed using the same basis functions as that of S^1, the degrees of freedom remains the same as that of S^0. Eqn.6.29 can be modified in the following manner so that it uses same basis functions and same number of degrees of freedom as that of S^1.

$$s = \mathbf{J}^1 \ [\mathbf{P}^1 \mathbf{Q}^1] \begin{bmatrix} \mathbf{p}^0 \\ \mathbf{q}^0 \end{bmatrix}, \quad (6.30)$$

where $\mathbf{q}^0$ is the collection of wavelet coefficients whose values are zero, $\mathbf{P}^1$ and $\mathbf{Q}^1$ are the synthesis matrices $\mathbf{P}^1_{lift}$ and $\mathbf{Q}^1_{lift}$ respectively. The above formulation yields a multiresolution representation of the control mesh S^1 obtained via one subdivision step on the previous control mesh S^0. The mesh S^1 is represented as a mesh at level 0 along with the detail (wavelet) coefficients at level 0. As mentioned earlier, these coefficients would become non-zero when the smooth limit surface deforms over time due to synthesized force application. Similarly after one more subdivision step, the new control mesh S^2 can be viewed as control vertex positions at level 0, wavelet coefficients at level 0 and wavelet coefficients at level 1, and can be written as

$$\begin{aligned} s &= \mathbf{J}^2 \ \mathbf{p}^2 \\ &= \mathbf{J}^2 \ [\mathbf{P}^2 \mathbf{Q}^2] \begin{bmatrix} \mathbf{p}^1 \\ \mathbf{q}^1 \end{bmatrix} \\ &= \mathbf{J}^2 \ [\mathbf{P}^2 \mathbf{Q}^2] \begin{bmatrix} \mathbf{P}^1 & \mathbf{Q}^1 & 0 \\ 0 & 0 & \mathbf{I} \end{bmatrix} \begin{bmatrix} \mathbf{p}^0 \\ \mathbf{q}^0 \\ \mathbf{q}^1 \end{bmatrix}, \quad (6.31) \end{aligned}$$

where $\mathbf{J}^2$ is the collection of basis functions at level 2, $\mathbf{p}^2$, $\mathbf{p}^1$ and $\mathbf{p}^0$ are the control vertex positions at level 2, 1 and 0 respectively, $\mathbf{q}^1$ and $\mathbf{q}^0$ are the wavelet coefficients at level 1 and 0 respectively, $\mathbf{I}$ is the identity matrix and $\mathbf{0}$ is the zero matrix. This idea can be generalized for a control mesh S^j obtained after j-th subdivision and the corresponding expression can be written as

$$\mathbf{s} = \mathbf{J}^j \ \mathbf{A}^j \ \mathbf{p}_r^j, \tag{6.32}$$

where $(\mathbf{p}_r^j)^T = [\mathbf{p}^0 \mathbf{q}^0 \dots \mathbf{q}^{j-2} \mathbf{q}^{j-1}]$, and

$$\mathbf{A}^j = [\mathbf{P}^j \mathbf{Q}^j] \begin{bmatrix} \mathbf{P}^{j-1} & \mathbf{Q}^{j-1} & \mathbf{0} \\ \mathbf{0} & \mathbf{0} & \mathbf{I} \end{bmatrix} \begin{bmatrix} \mathbf{P}^{j-2} & \mathbf{Q}^{j-2} & \mathbf{0} & \mathbf{0} \\ \mathbf{0} & \mathbf{0} & \mathbf{I} & \mathbf{I} \end{bmatrix} \dots \begin{bmatrix} \mathbf{P}^0 & \mathbf{Q}^0 & \mathbf{0} & \dots & \mathbf{0} \\ \mathbf{0} & \mathbf{0} & \mathbf{I} & \dots & \mathbf{I} \end{bmatrix}.$$

The multiresolution dynamics is developed using this formulation in the next section.

6.4 Dynamics

The smooth limit surface $\mathbf{s}$ can be made dynamic if the control vertex positions at level 0 and wavelet coefficients at level $1, 2, ..., (j-1)$ are functions of time. The velocity of the smooth surface, controlled by the mesh S^j obtained through j steps of model subdivision, is given by

$$\dot{\mathbf{s}}(\mathbf{x}, \mathbf{p}_r^j) = \mathbf{J}^j(\mathbf{x}) \mathbf{A}^j \dot{\mathbf{p}}_r^j, \tag{6.33}$$

where the overstruck dot denotes the time derivative and $\mathbf{x} \in S^j$. The Lagrangian motion equation (refer to Eqn.2.5) can be derived in a similar fashion as mentioned in earlier chapters, and is given by

$$\mathbf{M}^j \ddot{\mathbf{p}}_r^j + \mathbf{D}^j \dot{\mathbf{p}}_r^j + \mathbf{K}^j \mathbf{p}_r^p = \mathbf{f}_p^j, \tag{6.34}$$

where $\mathbf{M}^j$, $\mathbf{D}^j$ and $\mathbf{K}^j$ are the j-th level mass, damping and stiffness matrices respectively and $\mathbf{f}_p^j$ is the generalized force vector at level j. If $\mu(\mathbf{x})$ is the mass density of the subdivision surface model, then the mass matrix at j-th level is given by

$$\mathbf{M}^j = \int_{\mathbf{x} \in S^j} \mu(\mathbf{x}) (\mathbf{A}^j)^T (\mathbf{J}^j(\mathbf{x}))^T \mathbf{J}^j(\mathbf{x}) \mathbf{A}^j d\mathbf{x}.$$

The damping matrix $\mathbf{D}^j$ can be derived in a similar fashion, while the stiffness matrix $\mathbf{K}^j$ can be obtained following the techniques described in Section 4.3.2. The generalized force vector at level j can be written as

$$\mathbf{f}_p^j = \int_{\mathbf{x} \in S^j} (\mathbf{A}^j)^T (\mathbf{J}^j(\mathbf{x}))^T \mathbf{f}(\mathbf{x}, t) d\mathbf{x}.$$

6.5   Implementation Details

Multiresolution representation of the evolving control mesh achieves coarse-to-fine as well as fine-to-coarse manipulation of the smooth limit surface. For example, the user starts with a deformable smooth surface with a simple control mesh S^0 and directly manipulates the limit surface by applying synthesized forces. When an equilibrium is obtained, the user can increase the degrees of freedom by switching to

a control mesh S^1 which is theoretically obtained by applying one subdivision step

on S^0, but represented as a collection of vertex positions in S^0 along with wavelet

coefficients at level 0 needed to reconstruct S^1. The wavelet coefficients are zero at

the point of switching, but becomes non-zero as the control mesh S^1, represented

as mentioned above, evolves over time. The user can further increase the degrees

of freedom to obtain more localized effect by introducing control mesh S^2 which is

represented as control vertex positions of mesh S^0, along with wavelet coefficients

at level 0 and 1. Thus the user can have coarse-to-fine manipulation of the smooth

limit surface. This facility is also present in the multilevel dynamics approach as

mentioned earlier. However, the multilevel dynamics approach does not support fine-

to-coarse manipulation – it fails if the user wants to apply synthesized forces on a

coarser control mesh at level j after moving up to level $j + k$. This can be achieved

in multiresolution approach by simply using the dynamic equation of motion at level

j, and applying synthesized forces on a smooth limit surface which is obtained by

multiresolution synthesis using "time varying" control vertex positions at level 0

and wavelet coefficients at level $0, 1, \ldots, (j - 1)$ and "static" wavelet coefficients at

level $j, (j + 1), \ldots, (j + k - 1)$. If the user switches back to level $(j + k)$, then

the control vertex positions at level 0 as well as all the wavelet coefficients at level

$0, 1, \ldots, (j - 1), j, (j + 1), \ldots, (j + k - 1)$ become function of time, and the system

switches back to the motion equation of level $(j + k)$.

The actual implementation differs slightly from the formulation to achieve efficiency in coarse-to-fine and fine-to-coarse manipulation. In the implemented system, the user starts out with a smooth limit surface which has a simple control mesh with very few degrees of freedom. The model grows and when the equilibrium is achieved, one step of subdivision yields larger degrees of freedom. This larger degrees of freedom are the control vertex positions in this finer resolution and not control vertex positions in lower resolution along with wavelet coefficients in that lower resolution. The model can grow further, and if more subdivision step is needed to increase the degrees of freedom, it is handled in a similar fashion. If at any certain point of time the user needs to go back to a coarser level control mesh, wavelet decomposition is done on the higher resolution base mesh. This decomposition yields vertex positions in the coarser level mesh (which becomes the new base mesh) and non-zero wavelet coefficients. The lower resolution mesh evolves with time due to the force applied on the limit surface. It may be noted that the limit surface in this scenario is obtained by doing wavelet reconstruction with non-zero wavelet coefficients at some levels. The user can choose further coarser level control mesh by repeating the same process.

In the implemented system, the user can achieve global deformation on a detailed mesh by going down couple of levels using wavelet decomposition, retaining the wavelet coefficients, and applying force on the limit surface (obtained through wavelet reconstruction process) and letting the coarser level mesh evolve. Similarly, to achieve local deformation on a coarser mesh, the user can move up couple of steps by doing subdivision (and adding non-zero wavelet coefficients at higher levels, if present) and applying synthesized forces in the region of interest.

The formulation using wavelet representation has mathematical niceties, but inefficient for implementation purposes. The synthesized force is applied on the limit surface. To evaluate the limit surface, wavelet reconstruction needs to be done at each time step starting from the original control mesh upto a specified level if an explicit wavelet representation of the evolving control mesh is maintained as mentioned in the formulation. On the other hand, if the evolving mesh is control vertex positions at that resolution, then the wavelet reconstruction starts from that resolution for evaluating the limit surface. Wavelet decomposition needs to be done while going down from finer to coarser resolution, but this happens only once in a while, and not at each time step. Therefore, the implemented version is much more efficient. It may be noted that the motion equation at any level is implemented using finite element techniques discussed in earlier chapters for various subdivision schemes.

CHAPTER 7
SYSTEM ARCHITECTURE

The architecture of the prototype system is described in this chapter. The basic building blocks of the system are different modules performing different tasks. The overall architecture of the system is shown in Fig.7.1.

The user first provides the input about the geometry and topology of the initial mesh. Typically these information consist of some type of connectivity information and control vertex positions in 3D. The topological information processing module derives other necessary topological information from the given input data, and passes all the information to the subdivision module. The subdivision module performs pre-specified number of subdivision steps on the initial mesh, and then the finite element analysis module computes different elemental matrices needed by the update engine. The user can apply different types of synthesized forces on the limit surface, and the model is constantly updated to obtain an equilibrium position. The updated information is passed to the display module which renders the deforming smooth surface on the screen. The user is also allowed to choose different model parameter values like mass density, damping density, spring constants etc. Details of the specific modules are provided in the rest of this chapter.

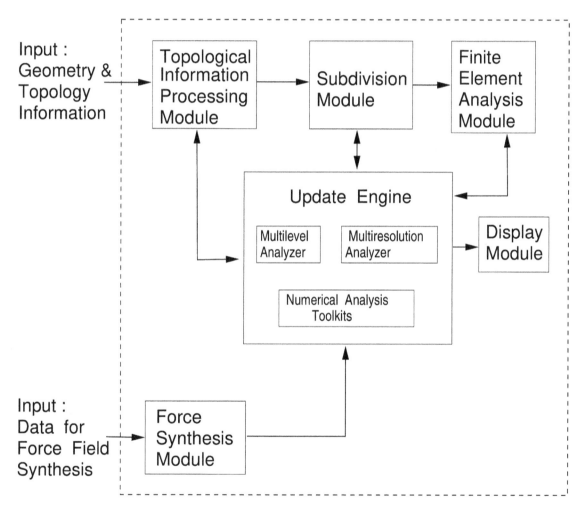

Figure 7.1. System architecture.

7.1 Topological Information Processing Module

In the implemented system, the user needs to provide the connectivity of the initial mesh by listing the vertices of every face. The vertex information of a face must be provided in an orderly fashion (either clockwise or anti-clockwise). The topological information processing module derives other necessary information like vertex connectivity information of the edges, edge connectivity information of the faces etc. from the input provided by the user.

7.2 Subdivision Module

This module applies different subdivision rules to refine an input control mesh. Currently, Catmull-Clark and modified butterfly subdivision schemes are supported in the system. Other subdivision schemes can also be easily incorporated. The subdivision scheme for a specific application is chosen by the user. However, there are certain inherent restrictions depending on the chosen subdivision scheme. For example, butterfly subdivision scheme can be chosen only if the initial (control) mesh has triangular faces. Once the user provides input about the initial mesh and the chosen subdivision scheme, this module then subdivides the initial mesh a pre-specified number of times to obtain a high resolution mesh which effectively approximates the smooth limit surface.

7.3 Finite Element Analysis Module

The finite element analysis module determines the type of finite element to be used and the total number of elements describing the smooth limit surface. It computes all elemental matrices such as mass, damping and stiffness matrices, as well as determines the set of vertices in the initial mesh controlling each individual element. This module also provides the information about the global mass, damping and stiffness matrices without actually assembling them from individual elemental matrices.

7.4   Force Synthesis Module

The user can apply various types of forces on the smooth limit surface. Currently spring forces, balloon forces, and image gradient-based forces are being supported. Other types of forces can also be easily incorporated. The user applies spring forces on the limit surface by providing points in 3D from which the springs need to be attached. The 3D point specification is done either interactively from mouse input or from files. To apply balloon forces, the user needs to specify whether the ballooning force is to inflate the model or to deflate the model. Volume images are provided as input to apply image gradient-based forces. A detailed discussion on these force application methods was provided in Section 3.3.4.

7.5   Update Engine

After the user provides all the necessary information about the model and the force application method, the update engine constantly updates the dynamic subdivision surface model to achieve an equilibrium position. The discretized second order differential equation of motion leads to solving a large sparse linear system of equations. Conjugate gradient [34, 75], an iterative linear system solver, is used for this purpose. The user can choose either multilevel dynamics or multiresolution dynamics approach, and the update engine accordingly chooses algorithms when the degrees of freedom of the evolving surface model is changed.

7.6   Display Module

The update engine constantly updates the dynamic model, and the relevant geometric and topological information is passed to the display module for rendering the evolving smooth surface. The display module uses OpenGL graphics libraries for rendering purposes. It also serves as the input module for mouse-based user interactions.

CHAPTER 8
APPLICATIONS

The proposed dynamic framework extends the application areas of subdivision surfaces beyond the traditional modeling domain. The framework enhances the suitability of subdivision surfaces for geometric modeling. At the same time, the proposed dynamic models can be used for recovery of shapes from range and volume data, non-rigid motion estimation, multiresolution editing and natural terrain modeling. The applicability of the dynamic model in these areas is further illustrated in the rest of this chapter.

8.1 Geometric Modeling

The proposed dynamic framework for subdivision surfaces can be used to represent a wide variety of arbitrary topological shapes with remarkable ease. In a typical geometric modeling application using dynamic subdivision surfaces, the user can specify any mesh as the initial (control) mesh, and the corresponding limit surface can be sculpted interactively by applying synthesized forces. Any dynamic subdivision surface model can be used for the modeling purpose. The examples shown in this section use dynamic Catmull-Clark and dynamic modified butterfly subdivision surface models.

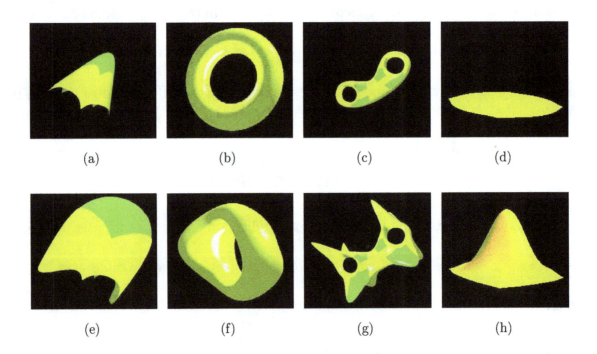

Figure 8.1. (a), (b), (c) and (d) : Initial shapes (obtained applying Catmull-Clark subdivision rules on control meshes); (e), (f), (g) and (h) : the corresponding modified shapes after interactive force application.

First, dynamic Catmull-Clark surface models as presented in Chapter 3 are used for shape modeling. The special elements in the limit surface are darkly shaded and the normal elements are lightly shaded in all the modeling examples. It may be noted that the formulation presented in Chapter 5, which will have only one type of finite element in the limit surface, can be used as well. In Fig.8.1, several initial surfaces obtained from different control meshes using Catmull-Clark subdivision rules and the corresponding modified surfaces after interactive spring force application are shown. To change the shape of an initial surface, springs are attached from different points in 3D to the nearest points on the limit surface such that the limit surface deforms towards these points generating the desired shape. In Fig.8.1(a), an open surface defined by an initial mesh of 61 vertices and 45 faces is shown. The mesh has one extraordinary vertex of degree 5. This limit surface is modified by applying spring forces interactively, and the modified surface is depicted in Fig.8.1(e). A torus, defined by an initial mesh of 32 vertices and 32 faces, and its modified shape is shown in Fig.8.1(b) and (f) respectively. The initial mesh of the smooth limit surface shown in Fig.8.1(c) has 544 faces and 542 vertices, 8 of them are extraordinary vertices of degree 5. The limit surface is modified interactively by applying spring forces from various points in 3D and the modified shape is depicted in Fig.8.1(g). Note that the extent of deformation has been interactively controlled by varying the stiffness of the attached springs. The upper portion of the limit surface has been deformed by applying spring forces of higher magnitude, whereas the lower portion has been modified by applying spring forces of lower magnitude. The spread of the

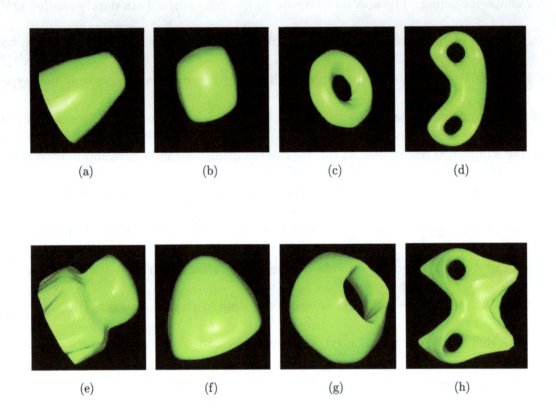

Figure 8.2. (a), (b), (c) and (d) : Initial shapes (obtained applying modified butterfly subdivision rules on control meshes); (e), (f), (g) and (h) : the corresponding modified shapes after interactive sculpting via force application.

deformation effect is clearly larger in the latter case for obvious reasons. Finally, a flat sheet defined by an initial mesh of 64 faces and 81 vertices, shown in Fig.8.1(d), is deformed interactively to obtain the hat-like shape shown in Fig.8.1(h).

Next, shape modeling examples using the dynamic modified butterfly subdivision surface model are shown. The limit surface here consists of a single type of smooth triangular finite element patches, irrespective of the number of extraordinary vertices in the control mesh. In Fig.8.2, several initial surfaces obtained from different control meshes using the modified butterfly subdivision rules and the corresponding modified surfaces after interactive sculpting are shown. As with the dynamic Catmull-Clark subdivision surfaces, the user can attach springs from different points in 3D to the nearest points on the limit surface and the limit surface deforms towards these points to generate the desired shape. The initial mesh of the smooth surface shown in Fig.8.2(a) has 125 faces and 76 vertices (degrees of freedom), which is deformed to the smooth shape shown in Fig.8.2(e) by interactive spring force application. The initial mesh of the closed cube-like shape in Fig.8.2(b) has 24 faces and 14 vertices. This cube-like shape is deformed to the shape shown in Fig.8.2(f). The one hole torus in Fig.8.2(c) and the corresponding modified shape in Fig.8.2(g) have initial meshes with 64 faces and 32 vertices. A two hole torus with a control mesh of 272 faces and 134 vertices, shown in Fig.8.2(d), is dynamically sculpted to the shape shown in Fig.8.2(h).

8.2   Shape Recovery from Range and Volume Data

The dynamic subdivision surface models can recover the underlying shape of a given range or volume data set in a hierarchical fashion. The initialized model deforms under the influence of the synthesized forces from the range or volume data. When an approximate shape is recovered, a new control mesh can be obtained by doing one step of subdivision on the initial mesh thereby increasing the degrees of freedom to represent the same limit surface, and a better fit to the given range data set can be achieved. It may be noted that the model initialization is interactive, and the initialized model can have any control mesh of the desired genus. However,

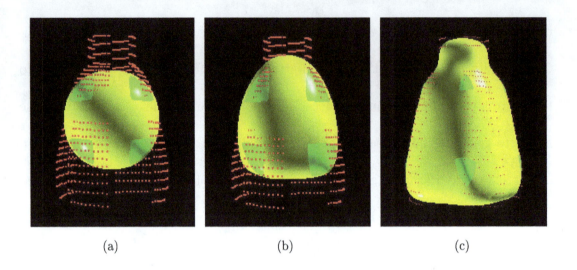

(a)   (b)   (c)

Figure 8.3. (a) Range data of a bulb along with the initialized model, (b) an intermediate stage of evolution, and (c) the fitted dynamic Catmull-Clark subdivision surface model.

an initial mesh with few degrees of freedom usually performs better in terms of the compact representation of the underlying shape.

Any dynamic subdivision surface model can be used for shape recovery. Next, three examples of shape recovery from range data sets are shown. The first two examples use dynamic Catmull-Clark subdivision surface model and the third one uses dynamic modified butterfly subdivision surface model. The error in fit, which is defined as the maximum distance between a data point and the nearest point on the limit surface as a percentage of the diameter of the smallest sphere enclosing the object, is approximately 3% in all the experiments with range data. The time of dynamic evolution for fitting the range data sets used in the experiments is approximately 3 minutes in a SGI O_2 workstation.

144

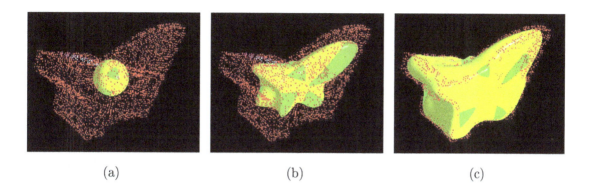

(a) (b) (c)

Figure 8.4. (a) Range data of an anvil along with the initialized model, (b) an intermediate stage of evolution, and (c) the fitted dynamic Catmull-Clark subdivision surface model.

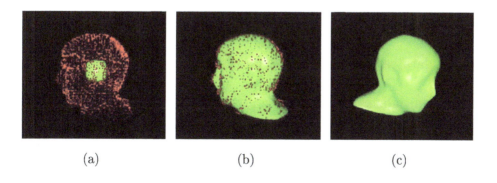

(a) (b) (c)

Figure 8.5. (a) Range data of a head along with the initialized model, (d) the fitted dynamic butterfly subdivision model, and (c) visualization of the shape from another view point.

The examples shown in Fig.8.3 and Fig.8.4 involve dynamic Catmull-Clark subdivision surface. The same shading convention for normal and special elements as mentioned earlier is used. In both of these examples, the initialized model had 96 faces and 98 vertices, 8 of them being extraordinary vertices of degree 3. The final fitted model, obtained through one step of subdivision, has a control polygon of 384 faces with 386 vertices. In Fig.8.3, the dynamic Catmull-Clark subdivision surface model is fitted to laser range data acquired from multiple views of a light bulb. Prior to applying the model fitting algorithm, the data were transformed into a single reference coordinate system. The model was initialized inside the 1000 range data points on the surface of the bulb. In the next experiment, the dynamic Catmull-Clark subdivision surface model is fitted to an anvil data set (Fig.8.4). The data set has 2031 data points. It may be noted that the final shape with 3% error tolerance uses very few control points for representation in comparison with the number of data points present in the original range data set.

In the last example with range data set, the shape of a human head is recovered from a range data set using dynamic modified butterfly subdivision surface model (Fig.8.5). The initialized model has a control mesh comprising of 24 triangular faces and 14 vertices whereas the control mesh of the fitted model has 384 triangular faces and 194 vertices. The range data set has 1779 points in 3D, and a compact representation of the recovered shape using few degrees of freedom in comparison with original data set is obtained in this example as well.

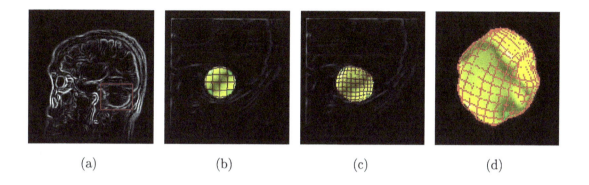

Figure 8.6. (a) A slice from a brain MRI, (b) initialized model inside the region of interest superimposed on the slice, (c) the fitted model superimposed on the slice, and (d) a 3D view of the dynamic Catmull-Clark subdivision surface model fitted to the cerebellum.

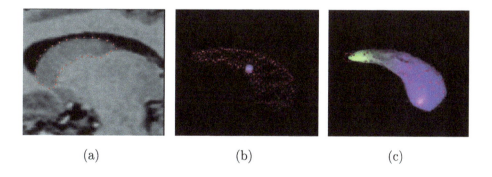

Figure 8.7. (a) Data points identifying the boundary of the caudate nucleus on a MRI slice of human brain, (b) data points (from all slices) in 3D along with the initialized model, and (c) the fitted dynamic butterfly subdivision model.

The application of the dynamic subdivision surface models to anatomical shape recovery from 3D volumetric MRI data is shown in the next two examples. The first one uses dynamic Catmull-Clark model and the next one uses dynamic modified butterfly subdivision surface model.

A dynamic Catmull-Clark subdivision surface model is fitted to a cerebellum (a cortical structure in brain) given an input of 30 sagittal slices from a MR brain scan. As in the examples with range data, the initialized model had 96 faces and 98 vertices, 8 of them being extraordinary vertices of degree 3. The final fitted model, obtained through one step of subdivision, has a control polygon of 384 faces with 386 vertices. Fig.8.6(a) depicts a slice from this MRI scan and the model initialization is shown in Fig.8.6(b). Continuous image based forces are applied to the model and the model deforms under the influence of these forces until maximum conformation to the boundaries of the desired cerebellum shape. The final fitted model is shown in Fig.8.6(c). A 3D view of the fitted model is depicted in Fig.8.6(d).

In the next example, the shape extraction of a caudate nucleus (another cortical structure in human brain) is presented from 64 MRI slices, each of size $(256, 256)$. Fig.8.7(a) depicts a slice from this MRI scan along with the points placed by an expert neuroscientist on the boundary of the shape of interest. Fig.8.7(b) depicts the interactively placed sparse set of data points (placed in some of the slices depicting the boundary of the shape of interest) in 3D along with the initialized model. Note that points had to be interactively placed on the boundary of the caudate nucleus in MR slices lacking image gradients which delineate the caudate from the surrounding tissue in the image. Continuous image-based forces as well as spring forces are applied to the model and the model deforms under the influence of these forces until maximum conformation to the boundaries of the desired caudate shape. The final fitted model in 3D is shown in Fig.8.7(c). The initialized dynamic butterfly subdivision surface model has a control mesh comprising of 24 triangular faces and 14 vertices whereas the control mesh of the fitted model has 384 triangular faces and 194 vertices.

8.3 Non-rigid Motion Estimation

The dynamic subdivision surface models can be used effectively to estimate the motion of a non-rigid object from a given time sequence of range or volume data. An example is shown in Fig.8.8 where the motion of the left-ventricular chamber of a canine heart is tracked over a complete cardiac cycle using dynamic modified butterfly subdivision surface model. The data set comprised of 16 3D CT images, with each volume image having 118 slices of 128×128 pixels. First, the shape is recovered from one data set using image-based (gradient) as well as point-based forces. As before, the initialized model has a control mesh comprising of 24 triangular faces and 14 vertices whereas the control mesh of the fitted model has 384 triangular faces and 194 vertices. Once the shape is recovered from one data set, this fitted model is used as an initialization for the next data set to track the shape of interest. The snapshots from motion tracking are shown in Fig.8.8 for the 16 volume data sets. It may be noted that the control mesh describing the smooth surfaces shown in Fig.8.8 has only 384 triangular faces with a total of 194 vertices as mentioned earlier. This experiment clearly shows that our model can be used to track a shape of interest

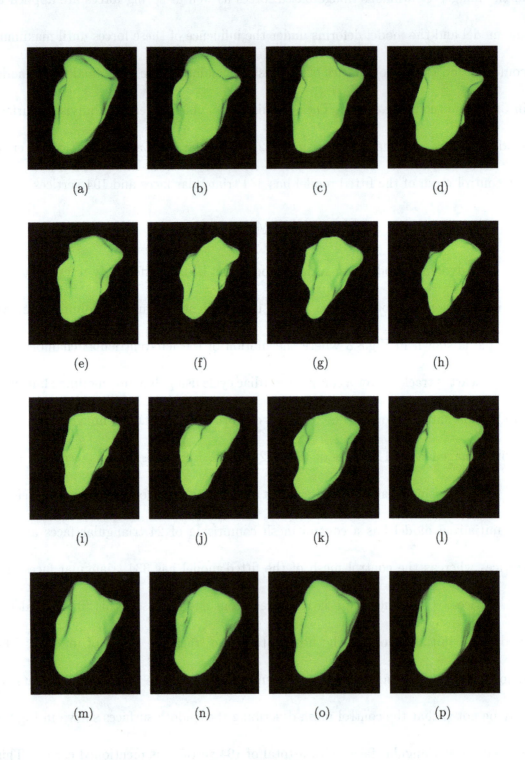

Figure 8.8. Snapshots from the animation of canine heart motion over a cardiac cycle using the dynamic butterfly subdivision model.

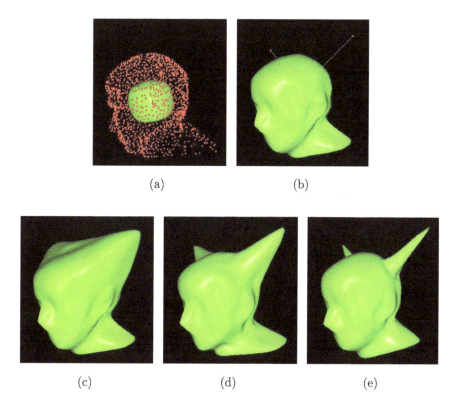

Figure 8.9. (a) The initialized model along with the data set; (b) the fitted model with two subdivisions on the initial mesh, along with attached springs for editing. The model after editing (c) at lower resolution, (d) at the same resolution of the fitted model, and (e) at higher resolution.

from a set of time dependent volume data sets in an efficient manner. Note that no other existing purely geometric subdivision surface technique can be used with (time varying) continuous data sets.

8.4 Multiresolution Editing

The proposed dynamic subdivision techniques present hierarchical shape recovery and shape modeling within a common framework, where the modeler can scan in 3D data points of a prototype model, recover the underlying shape from the point set, and then edit the recovered shape. The multiresolution representation of the evolving control mesh as presented in Chapter 6 enables the modeler to edit the smooth limit surface at any desired level. Within the proposed multiresolution dynamic framework, the modeler does not need to build a model from scratch (unlike other shape modeling techniques), and there is no need of using computationally intensive remeshing techniques for multiresolution representation (unlike other shape recovery techniques). The idea is illustrated in Fig.8.9, where the shape of a head is first recovered from a range data set and then edited at various levels using spring forces from two points in 3D. The effect was more global in the lowest level edited, and the effect became increasingly local as the level of editing was increased.

8.5   Natural Terrain Modeling

In this section, a novel technique for synthesizing realistic terrain models from elevation data is developed by using the dynamic finite element method-based subdivision surface model for surface reconstruction, and a variant of the successive random addition method for fractal surface synthesis. Roughness is an essential characteristic of the natural terrains and hence traditional surface reconstruction methods using smoothness constraints do not yield the desired results. Fournier et al. [33] first proposed a random displacement technique for synthesizing fractal surfaces which was later modified by Saupe [84] in his successive random addition scheme of generating fractals. Yokoya et al. [107] improved these schemes by adding data constraints. Szeliski and Terzopoulos [94] proposed constrained fractal surfaces using a Gibbs sampler algorithm which was later improved by Vemuri et al. [102, 103]. Arakawa and Krotkov [1] refined the original Gibbs sampler technique by redefining the temperature (control) parameter to obtain better control of roughness in the fitted (constrained) fractal surface. However, the (CPU) execution times reported in their work are very high, thus making their scheme unattractive for many applications.

All the techniques for natural terrain modeling mentioned above usually needs a grid of very large size to model realistic terrains, especially with irregularly spaced data. Rümelin [82] developed an interesting fractal interpolation algorithm which can generate interpolating fractal surfaces for regularly or irregularly spaced data. However, this scheme is computationally intensive for large problems as pointed out in Vemuri et al. [103].

The subdivision schemes produce a smooth surface in the limit, and hence they are not suitable for synthesizing natural terrains which are rough. A scheme is developed in this dissertation using a variant of the successive random addition method [84] such that the limit surface looks like "natural" terrain. In the original successive random addition technique, an equally spaced rectangular grid is refined by interpolating the midpoints of each rectangular cell (thereby dividing each rectangular cell into four rectangular cells) and then all grid positions are perturbed by addition of a Gaussian noise. This process is carried out recursively to obtain a fractal surface whose roughness is controlled by the variance of the added Gaussian noise at different refinement levels. In this dissertation, *the butterfly subdivision scheme has been modified where vertex positions at various levels of subdivision are perturbed*

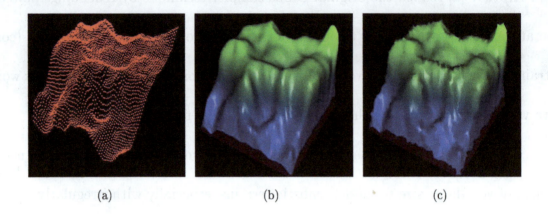

(a)   (b)   (c)

Figure 8.10. (a) Discrete elevation data set (4096 points), (b) fitted dynamic butterfly subdivision surface model with 841 vertices (without noise addition), and (c) fitted dynamic subdivision surface model with 841 vertices when Gaussian noise is added.

by addition of a Gaussian noise whose variance controls the roughness of the resulting limit surface. This process of Gaussian noise addition is similar to that of the successive random addition method mentioned earlier, the difference being the vertex positions obtained using butterfly subdivision rules are perturbed instead of grid points obtained through midpoint interpolation.

Two natural terrain synthesis results using dynamic modified butterfly subdivision surface model are presented in this section. The initialized model is deformed by applying spring forces on its limit surface from the discrete data points. At each time step, every control vertex position is perturbed by adding a random noise drawn from a Gaussian distribution. The variance of the Gaussian distribution determines the roughness of the synthesized surface. In both the examples, the initialized butterfly subdivision model has an initial (control) mesh with 98 triangular faces and 68 control vertices. The "natural" looking limit surface of the initialized model is

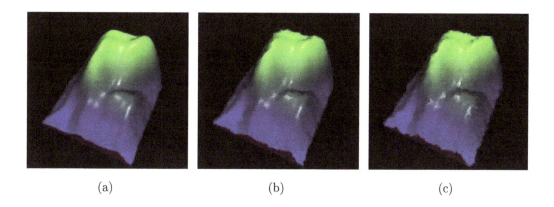

(a) (b) (c)

Figure 8.11. Synthesized natural terrain of different roughness using the dynamic butterfly subdivision surface model with 841 vertices from a data set of 3099 elevation values.

deformed by the forces exerted from the discrete elevation data points. When an approximate fit is obtained, the model is subdivided to obtain a closer fit using more degrees of freedom (control vertices) of the new initial mesh. The fitted surface has 1568 triangular faces and 841 control vertices in both the experiments. It may be noted that synthesis of same quality natural terrains using the existing techniques requires a large number of grid points (of the order of 10^5) [1, 82, 94, 103] and hence the proposed technique provides a more compact representation of the synthesized terrain. The elevation data values are scaled to fit an unit cube and the variance of added noise is 10^{-4} for the synthesized fractal surface depicted in Fig.8.10. The corresponding value of noise variance for fractal surfaces depicted in Fig.8.11(a), (b) and (c) are 10^{-6}, 10^{-5} and 10^{-4} respectively. In the first experiment, 4096 elevation data points are used whereas the second data set comprised of 3099 elevation values. The error in fit is approximately 1% in both the examples.

CHAPTER 9
CONCLUSIONS AND FUTURE WORK

In this chapter, the contributions of this dissertation are summarized. Future research directions of the deformable subdivision surface model are also discussed.

9.1   Conclusions

In this dissertation, a dynamic framework has been developed for subdivision surfaces. This dynamic framework enhances the applicability of subdivision surfaces in geometric modeling applications where the modeler can directly and intuitively manipulate the smooth limit surface using synthesized forces. The proposed framework is very useful for hierarchical shape recovery from large range and volume data sets, as well as for non-rigid motion tracking from a temporal sequence of data sets. Multiresolution representation of the initial mesh controlling the smooth limit surface enables global and local editing of the shape as desired by the modeler. A novel technique for synthesizing natural terrain models from sparse elevation data using the dynamic framework in conjunction with a variant of the successive random addition technique has also been presented in this dissertation.

Several theoretical contributions has also been made in this dissertation. Local parameterization techniques suitable for embedding the geometric subdivision surface model in a physics-based modeling framework has been developed. Specific local parameterization techniques have been fully worked out for Catmull-Clark, modified butterfly and Loop subdivision schemes. Techniques for assigning material properties to geometric subdivision surfaces have been derived, motion equation for the dynamic model has been formulated, advantages of deformable models are incorporated into conventional subdivision schemes, dynamic hierarchical control has been introduced, multiresolution representation of the control mesh is derived and an unified approach for deriving subdivision surface-based finite elements has been presented.

The proposed dynamic framework has a promising future in computer graphics, geometric modeling and scientific visualization. Furthermore, the finite element techniques proposed in this dissertation should be of great interest to the engineering design and analysis community as well.

9.2 Future Directions

The proposed dynamic framework enhances the applicability of the subdivision surfaces in various applications, but still there are lots of research need to be done to meet the growing demands of modeling and other applications. In the rest of this section, several key issues needing attention are discussed.

9.2.1 Automatic Change of Topology

In the current framework, the evolving model can not change its topology if needed. Automatic change of topology for dynamic subdivision surface models is a very challenging and important research topic. The topologically adaptable deformable models developed by Malladi et al. [54] and McInerney and Terzopoulos

[63] can provide some insight about how to deal with topology changing in deformable subdivision surface models.

9.2.2 Local Refinement

In some applications, especially in shape recovery, it is more meaningful to locally refine the smooth limit surface, i.e., introduction of new degrees of freedom only in the regions where more details need to be recovered. Currently, this refinement is global where new degrees of freedom is introduced throughout the smooth limit surface. Local refinement implies distribution of degrees of freedom at a number of subdivision levels instead of one particular subdivision level. This is a very challenging but important research issue.

9.2.3 Automatic Model Parameter Selection

The model parameters like mass, damping, rigidity, bending are selected by the user in the current implementation. The choice of force constants and time step is also manual. Numerical stability of the deforming model is very sensitive to the choice of the parameter values. Research needs to be done on how to select these parameters automatically in different applications.

9.2.4 Constraint Imposition

In some applications, there might be a need to impose geometric as well functional constraints on the dynamic subdivision surface models. Position and normal constraints are examples of possible constraints. It is somewhat easier to impose these constraints on interpolatory dynamic subdivision surface models, but considerable research efforts need to be put for constraint imposition in the case of approximating dynamic subdivision surface models.

9.2.5 Recovery of Sharp Features

Recovery of sharp features using dynamic subdivision surface models is an open research problem. Even though piecewise smooth subdivision surfaces [40] has been developed, incorporating sharp features in a physically meaningful way for an evolving subdivision surface model is a challenging research issue.

9.2.6 Automatic Model Initialization

Currently model initialization is interactive. However, automatic model initialization techniques have been recently proposed by Delingette [24]. Similar techniques for deformable subdivision surface initialization need to be developed.

9.2.7 Improved Synthesized Force Fields

Recently Xu and Prince [106] have proposed new type of force fields which makes the model insensitive to the initialization. It would be nice to incorporate these force fields in the current system for better performance in the model fitting context.

REFERENCES

[1] K. Arakawa and E. Krotkov, "Fractal surface reconstruction for modeling natural terrain," in *Proceedings of the Conference on Computer Vision and Pattern Recognition*, pp. 314 – 320, 1993.

[2] A. Arneodo, E. Bacry and J.F. Muzy, "Solving the inverse fractal problem from wavelet analysis," *Europhysics Letters*, vol. 25, no. 7, pp. 479 – 484, March, 1994.

[3] A.A. Ball and D.J.T. Storry, "Conditions for tangent plane continuity over recursively generated B-spline surfaces," *ACM Transactions on Graphics*, vol. 7, no. 2, pp. 83 – 102, 1988.

[4] A.A. Ball and D.J.T. Storry, "An investigation of curvature variations over recursively generated B-spline surfaces," *ACM Transactions on Graphics*, vol. 9, no. 4, pp. 424 – 437, 1990.

[5] E. Bardinet, L.D. Cohen and N. Ayache, "Superquadrics and free-form deformations : A global model to fit and track 3D medical data," in *Lecture Notes in Computer Science, CVRMed'95*, N. Ayache, Ed., vol. 905, pp. 319 – 326, Springer - Verlag, Berlin, Germany, 1995.

[6] D.F. Berman, J.T. Bartell and D.H. Salesin, "Multiresolution painting and compositing," in *Computer Graphics Proceedings*, ACM SIGGRAPH, Annual Conference Series, pp. 85 – 90, July, 1994.

[7] G. Beylkin, R. Coifman and V. Rokhlin, "Fast wavelet transforms and numerical algorithms," *Communications on Pure and Applied Mathematics*, vol. 44, pp. 141 – 183, 1991.

[8] M.I.J. Bloor and M.J. Wilson, "Representing PDE surfaces in terms of B-splines," *Computer Aided Design*, vol. 22, no. 6, pp. 324 – 331, 1990.

[9] M.I.J. Bloor and M.J. Wilson, "Using partial differential equations to generate free-form surfaces," *Computer Aided Design*, vol. 22, no. 4, pp. 202 – 212, 1990.

[10] E. Catmull and J. Clark, "Recursively generated B-spline surfaces on arbitrary topological meshes," *Computer Aided Design*, vol. 10, no. 6, pp. 350 – 355, 1978.

[11] G. Celniker and D. Gossard, "Deformable curve and surface finite elements for free-form shape design," in *Computer Graphics Proceedings*, ACM SIGGRAPH, Annual Conference Series, pp. 257 – 266, July, 1991.

[12] G. Celniker and W. Welch, "Linear constraints for deformable B-spline surfaces," in *Proceedings of the Symposium on Interactive 3D Graphics*, pp. 165 – 170. ACM, New York, 1992.

[13] A. Certain, J. Popovic, T. DeRose, T. Duchamp, D.H. Salesin and W. Stuetzle, "Interactive multiresolution surface viewing," in *Computer Graphics Proceedings*, ACM SIGGRAPH, Annual Conference Series, pp. 91 – 98, August, 1996.

[14] G.M. Chaikin, "An algorithm for high speed curve generation," *Computer Vision, Graphics and Image Processing*, vol. 3, no. 4, pp. 346 – 349, 1974.

[15] Y. Chen and G. Medioni, "Surface description of complex objects from multiple range images," in *Proceedings of the Conference on Computer Vision and Pattern Recognition*, Seattle,WA, pp. 153 – 158, June, 1994.

[16] P.H. Christensen, E.J. Stollnitz, D.H. Salesin and T. DeRose, "Wavelet radiance," in *Proceedings of the Fifth Eurographics Workshop on Rendering*, Darmstadt, Germany, pp. 287 – 302, 1994.

[17] P.H. Christensen, E.J. Stollnitz, D.H. Salesin and T. DeRose, "Global illumination of glossy environments using wavelets and importance," *ACM Transactions on Graphics*, vol. 15, no. 1, pp. 37 – 71, January, 1996.

[18] C.K. Chui, *Wavelet analysis and its applications*, Academic Press, Boston, 1992.

[19] C.K. Chui and E. Quak, "Wavelets on a bounded interval," in *Numerical methods in approximation theory*, D. Braess and L.L. Schumaker, Eds., vol. 9, pp. 53 – 75, Birkhauser Verlag, Basel, 1992.

[20] A. Cohen, I. Daubechies and J.C. Feauveau, "Biorthogonal bases of compactly supported wavelets," *Communications on Pure and Applied Mathematics*, vol. 45, no. 5, pp. 485 – 560, 1992.

[21] L.D. Cohen and I. Cohen, "Finite-element methods for active contour models and balloons for 2D and 3D images," *IEEE Transactions on Pattern Analysis and Machine Intelligence*, vol. 15, no. 11, pp. 1131 – 1147, November, 1993.

[22] I. Daubechies, "Orthonormal bases of compactly supported wavelets," *Communications on Pure and Applied Mathematics*, vol. 41, no. 7, pp. 909 – 996, 1988.

[23] I. Daubechies, *Ten lectures on wavelets*, SIAM, Philadelphia, 1992.

[24] H. Delingette, "Initialization of deformable models from 3D data," in *Proceedings of the International Conference on Computer Vision*, Bombay, India, pp. 311 – 316, January, 1998.

[25] T. DeRose, M. Kass and T. Truong, "Subdivision surfaces in character animation," in *Computer Graphics Proceedings*, ACM SIGGRAPH, Annual Conference Series, pp. 85 – 94, July, 1998.

[26] R. DeVore, B. Jawerth and B. Lucier, "Image compression through wavelet transform coding," *IEEE Transactions on Information Theory*, vol. 38, no. 2, pp. 719 – 746, March, 1992.

[27] D. Doo, "A subdivision algorithm for smoothing down irregularly shaped polyhedrons," in *Proceedings on Interactive Techniques in Computer Aided Design*, pp. 157 – 165, 1978.

[28] D. Doo and M. Sabin, "Analysis of the behavior of recursive division surfaces near extraordinary points," *Computer Aided Design*, vol. 10, no. 6, pp. 356 – 360, 1978.

[29] N. Dyn, S. Hed and D. Levin, "Subdivision schemes for surface interpolation," in *Workshop in Computational Geometry*, A. Conte. et al., Ed., pp. 97 – 118, 1993.

[30] N. Dyn, D. Levin and J.A. Gregory, "A butterfly subdivision scheme for surface interpolation with tension control," *ACM Transactions on Graphics*, vol. 9, no. 2, pp. 160 – 169, April, 1990.

[31] A. Finkelstein, C.E. Jacobs and D.H. Salesin, "Multiresolution video," in *Computer Graphics Proceedings*, ACM SIGGRAPH, Annual Conference Series, pp. 281 – 290, August, 1996.

[32] A. Finkelstein and D.H. Salesin, "Multiresolution curves," in *Computer Graphics Proceedings*, ACM SIGGRAPH, Annual Conference Series, pp. 261 – 268, July, 1994.

[33] A. Fournier, D. Fussel, and L. Carpenter, "Computer rendering of stochastic models," *Communications of the ACM*, vol. 25, no. 6, pp. 371–384, 1982.

[34] G.H. Golub and V.H. Van Loan, *Matrix Computations*, The Johns Hopkins University Press, Baltimore, 1989.

[35] S.J. Gortler, P. Schröder, M.F. Cohen and P. Hanrahan, "Wavelet radiosity," in *Computer Graphics Proceedings*, ACM SIGGRAPH, Annual Conference Series, pp. 221 – 230, August, 1993.

[36] B.R. Gossick, *Hamilton's Principle and Physical Systems*, Academic Press, New York, 1967.

[37] A. Habib and J. Warren, "Edge and vertex insertion for a class of C^1 subdivision surfaces," *Computer Aided Geometric Design*, to appear.

[38] M. Halstead, M. Kass and T. DeRose, "Efficient, fair interpolation using Catmull-Clark surfaces," in *Computer Graphics Proceedings*, ACM SIGGRAPH, Annual Conference Series, pp. 35 – 44, August, 1993.

[39] H. Hoppe, *Surface reconstruction from unorganized points*, Ph.D. thesis, University of Washington, Seattle, 1994.

[40] H. Hoppe, T. DeRose, T. Duchamp, M. Halstead, H. Jin, J. McDonald, J. Schweitzer and W. Stuetzle, "Piecewise smooth surface reconstruction," in *Computer Graphics Proceedings*, ACM SIGGRAPH, Annual Conference Series, pp. 295 – 302, July, 1994.

[41] W.C. Huang and D. Goldgof, "Adaptive-size physically-based models for nonrigid motion analysis," in *Proceedings of the Conference on Computer Vision and Pattern Recognition*, Urbana-Champaign, IL, pp. 833 – 835, June, 1992.

[42] H. Kardestuncer, *The Finite Element Handbook*, McGraw-Hill, New York, 1987.

[43] L. Kobbelt, "Interpolatory refinement by variational methods," in *Approximation Theory VIII*, C. Chui and L. Schumaker, Eds., vol. 2 of *Wavelets and Multilevel Approximation*, pp. 217 – 224, World Scientific Publishing Co., 1995.

[44] L. Kobbelt, "A variational approach to subdivision," *Computer-Aided Geometric Design*, vol. 13, pp. 743 – 761, 1996.

[45] L. Kobbelt, S. Campagna, J. Vorsatz and H.P. Seidel, "Interactive multiresolution modeling on arbitrary meshes," in *Computer Graphics Proceedings*, ACM SIGGRAPH, Annual Conference Series, pp. 105 – 114, July, 1998.

[46] L. Kobbelt and P. Schröder, "Constructing variationally optimal curves through subdivision," Tech. Rep. CS-TR-97-05, California Institute of Technology Computer Science Department Technical Report, 1997.

[47] E. Koh, D. Metaxas and N. Badler, "Hierarchical shape representation using locally adaptive finite elements," in *Lecture Notes in computer Science, Computer Vision - ECCV'94*, J.O. Eklundh, Ed., vol. 800, pp. 441 – 446, Springer-Verlag, Berlin, Germany, 1994.

[48] S.H. Lai and B.C. Vemuri, "Physically-based adaptive preconditioning for early vision," *IEEE Transactions on Pattern Analysis and Machine Intelligence*, vol. 19, no. 6, pp. 594 – 607, June, 1997.

[49] F. Leitner and P. Cinquin, "Complex topology 3D objects segmentation," in *Model-based Vision Development and Tools, SPIE Proceedings*, Bellingham, WA, vol. 1609, pp. 16 – 26, SPIE, 1991.

[50] Z. Liu, S.J. Gortler and M.F. Cohen, "Hierarchical spacetime control," in *Computer Graphics Proceedings*, ACM SIGGRAPH, Annual Conference Series, pp. 35 – 42, July, 1994.

[51] C. Loop, *Smooth subdivision surfaces based on triangles*, M.S. thesis, University of Utah, Department of Mathematics, 1987.

[52] J.M. Lounsbery, *Multiresolution analysis for surfaces of arbitrary topological type*, Ph.D. thesis, University of Washington, Seattle, 1994.

[53] J.M. Lounsbery, T. DeRose and J. Warren, "Multiresolution analysis for surfaces of arbitrary topological type," *ACM Transactions on Graphics*, vol. 16, no. 1, pp. 34 – 73, January, 1997.

[54] R. Malladi, J.A. Sethian, and B.C. Vemuri, "Shape modeling with front propagation : a level set approach," *IEEE Transactions on Pattern Analysis and Machine Intelligence*, vol. 17, no. 2, pp. 158 – 175, February, 1995.

[55] S. Mallat, "A theory for multiresolution signal decomposition : the wavelet representation," *IEEE Transactions on Pattern Analysis and Machine Intelligence*, vol. 11, no. 7, pp. 674 – 693, July, 1989.

[56] S. Mallat and W.L. Hwang, "Singularity detection and processing with wavelets," *IEEE Transactions on Information Theory*, vol. 38, no. 2, pp. 617 – 643, March, 1992.

[57] C. Mandal, H. Qin and B.C. Vemuri, "Dynamic smooth subdivision surfaces for data visualization," in *IEEE Visualization'97 Conference Proceedings*, Phoenix,AZ, pp. 371 – 377, October, 1997.

[58] C. Mandal, H. Qin and B.C. Vemuri, "Direct manipulation of butterfly subdivision surfaces : a physics-based approach," *IEEE Transactions on Visualization and Computer Graphics*, submitted, available as University of Florida Tech. Rep. CISE-TR-98-009, 1998.

[59] C. Mandal, H. Qin and B.C. Vemuri, "A novel FEM-based dynamic framework for subdivision surfaces," *Fifth ACM Symposium on Solid Modeling and Applications*, submitted, 1999.

[60] C. Mandal, B.C. Vemuri and H. Qin, "Shape recovery using dynamic subdivision surfaces," in *Proceedings of the International Conference on Computer Vision*, Bombay, India, pp. 805 – 810, January, 1998.

[61] C. Mandal, B.C. Vemuri and H. Qin, "A new dynamic FEM-based subdivision surface model for shape recovery and tracking in medical images," in *Lecture Notes in computer Science, Medical Image Computing and Computer-Assisted Intervention - MICCAI'98*, W.M. Wells et al., Eds., Cambridge, MA, vol. 1496, pp. 753 – 760, Springer, 1998.

[62] T. McInerney and D. Terzopoulos, "A dynamic finite element surface model for segmentation and tracking in multidimensional medical images with application to cardiac 4D image analysis," *Computerized Medical Imaging and Graphics*, vol. 19, no. 1, pp. 69 – 83, 1995.

[63] T. McInerney and D. Terzopoulos, "Topologically adaptable snakes," in *Proceedings of the International Conference on Computer Vision*, Cambridge, MA, pp. 840 – 845, June, 1995.

[64] T. McInerney and D. Terzopoulos, "Deformable models in medical image analysis : a survey," *Medical Image Analysis*, vol. 1, no. 2, pp. 91 – 108, 1996.

[65] D. Metaxas and D. Terzopoulos, "Dynamic deformation of solid primitives with constraints," in *Computer Graphics Proceedings*, ACM SIGGRAPH, Annual Conference Series, pp. 309 – 312, July, 1992.

[66] D. Metaxas and D. Terzopoulos, "Shape and non-rigid motion estimation through physics-based synthesis," *IEEE Transactions on Pattern Analysis and Machine Intelligence*, vol. 15, no. 6, pp. 580 – 591, June, 1993.

[67] D. Meyers, "Multiresolution tiling," in *Proceedings of Graphics Interface*, pp. 25 – 32, May, 1994.

[68] D. Meyers, *Reconstruction of surfaces from planar contours*, Ph.D. thesis, University of Washington, Seattle, 1994.

[69] O. Monga and R. Deriche, "3D edge detection using recursive filtering," in *Proceedings of IEEE Conference on Computer Vision and Pattern Recognition*, pp. 28 – 35, June, 1989.

[70] A. Pentland, "Fast solutions to physical equilibrium and interpolation problems," *Visual Computer*, vol. 8, no. 5-6, pp. 303 – 314, June, 1992.

[71] A. Pentland and B. Horowitz, "Recovery of non-rigid motion and structure," *IEEE Transactions on Pattern Analysis and Machine Intelligence*, vol. 13, no. 7, pp. 730 – 742, July, 1991.

[72] A. Pentland and J. Williams, "Good vibrations : Modal dynamics for graphics and animation," in *Computer Graphics Proceedings*, ACM SIGGRAPH, Annual Conference Series, pp. 215 – 222, 1989.

[73] J. Peters and U. Reif, "The simplest subdivision scheme for smoothing polyhedra," *ACM Transactions on Graphics*, vol. 16, no. 4, pp. 420 – 431, October, 1997.

[74] J. Peters and U. Reif, "Analysis of generalized B-spline subdivision algorithms," *SIAM Journal of Numerical Analysis*, to appear, available at ftp://ftp.cs.purdue.edu/pub/jorg/9697agb.ps.Z.

[75] W.H. Press, S.A. Teukolsky, W.T. Vetterling and B.P. Flannery, *Numerical Recipes in C*, Cambridge University Press, 1992.

[76] H. Qin, C. Mandal and B.C. Vemuri, "Dynamic Catmull-Clark subdivision surfaces," *IEEE Transactions on Visualization and Computer Graphics*, vol. 4, no. 3, pp. 215 – 229, July - September, 1998.

[77] H. Qin and D. Terzopoulos, "Dynamic NURBS swung surfaces for physics-based shape design," *Computer-Aided Design*, vol. 27, no. 2, pp. 111 – 127, 1995.

[78] H. Qin and D. Terzopoulos, "D-NURBS : A physics-based framework for geometric design," *IEEE Transactions on Visualization and Computer Graphics*, vol. 2, no. 1, pp. 85 – 96, January - March, 1996.

[79] E. Quak and N. Weyrich, "Decomposition and reconstruction algorithms for spline wavelets on a bounded interval," CAT report 294, Center for Approximation Theory, Texas A&M University, April, 1993.

[80] U. Reif, "A unified approach to subdivision algorithms near extraordinary points," *Computer Aided Geometric Design*, vol. 12 , no. 2, pp. 153 – 174, 1995.

[81] O. Rioul and M. Vetterli, "Wavelets and signal processing," *IEEE Signal Processing Magazine*, vol. 8, no. 4, pp. 14 – 38, October, 1991.

[82] W. Rümelin, "Fractal interpolation of random fields of fractional Brownian motion," in *Fractal Geometry and Computer Graphics*, J.L. Encarnacao et al., Eds., pp. 122 – 132, Springer-Verlag, 1992.

[83] M. Sabin, *The use of piecewise forms for the numerical representation of shape*, Ph.D. thesis, Hungarian Academy of Sciences, Budapest, 1976.

[84] D. Saupe, "Algorithms for random fractals," in *The Science of Fractal Images*, H.O. Peitgen and D. Saupe, Eds., pp. 71 – 136, Springer - Verlag, 1988.

[85] P. Schröder, S.J. Gortler, M.F. Cohen and P. Hanrahan, "Wavelet projections for radiosity," in *Proceedings of the Fourth Eurographics Workshop on Rendering*, Paris, France, pp. 105 – 114, 1994.

[86] P. Schröder and W. Sweldens, "Spherical wavelets : efficiently representing functions on the sphere," in *Computer Graphics Proceedings*, ACM SIGGRAPH, Annual Conference Series, pp. 161 – 172, August, 1995.

[87] J.E. Schweitzer, *Analysis and Application of Subdivision Surfaces*, Ph.D. thesis, University of Washington, Seattle, 1996.

[88] T.W. Sederberg, J. Zheng, D. Sewell and M. Sabin, "Non-uniform recursive subdivision surfaces," in *Computer Graphics Proceedings*, ACM SIGGRAPH, Annual Conference Series, pp. 387 – 394, July, 1998.

[89] L.H. Staib and J.S. Duncan, "Boundary finding with parametrically deformable models," *IEEE Transactions on Pattern Analysis and Machine Intelligence*, vol. 14, no. 11, pp. 1061 – 1075, 1992.

[90] J. Stam, "Exact evaluation of Catmull-Clark subdivision surfaces at arbitrary parameter values," in *Computer Graphics Proceedings*, ACM SIGGRAPH, Annual Conference Series, pp. 395 – 404, July, 1998.

[91] J. Stam, "Evaluation of Loop Subdivision Surfaces," in *SIGGRAPH'98 CDROM Proceedings*, ACM SIGGRAPH, July, 1998.

[92] E.J. Stollnitz, T.D. DeRose and D.H. Salesin, *Wavelets for computer graphics : theory and applications*, Morgan Kaufmann, San Francisco, 1996.

[93] W. Sweldens, "The lifting scheme : a custom-design construction of biorthogonal wavelets," Tech. Rep. 1994:7, Industrial Mathematics Initiative, Department of Mathematics, University of South Carolina, 1994.

[94] R. Szeliski and D. Terzopoulos, "From splines to fractals," in *Computer Graphics Proceedings*, ACM SIGGRAPH, Annual Conference Series, pp. 51 – 60, August, 1989.

[95] H. Tanaka and F. Kishino, "Adaptive mesh generation for surface reconstruction : Parallel hierarchical triangulation without discontinuities," in *Proceedings of the Conference on Computer Vision and Pattern Recognition*, New York City, NY, pp. 88 – 94, June, 1993.

[96] D. Terzopoulos, "Regularization of inverse visual problems involving discontinuities," *IEEE Transactions on Pattern Analysis and Machine Intelligence*, vol. 8, no. 4, pp. 413 – 424, 1986.

[97] D. Terzopoulos and K. Fleischer, "Deformable models," *The Visual Computer*, vol. 4, no. 6, pp. 306 – 331, 1988.

[98] D. Terzopoulos and D. Metaxas, "Dynamic 3D models with local and global deformations: Deformable superquadrics," *IEEE Transactions on Pattern Analysis and Machine Intelligence*, vol. 13, no. 7, pp. 703 – 714, July, 1991.

[99] D. Terzopoulos, J. Platt, A. Barr and K. Fleischer, "Elastically deformable models," in *Computer Graphics Proceedings*, ACM SIGGRAPH, Annual Conference Series, pp. 205 – 214, 1987.

[100] D. Terzopoulos and H. Qin, "Dynamic NURBS with geometric constraints for interactive sculpting," *ACM Transactions on Graphics*, vol. 13, no. 2, pp. 103 – 136, April, 1994.

[101] M. Vasilescu and D. Terzopoulos, "Adaptive meshes and shells : Irregular triangulation, discontinuities and hierarchical subdivision," in *Proceedings of the*